The Longest Afternoon

The Longest Afternoon

The 400 Men who Decided the
Battle of Waterloo

BRENDAN SIMMS

BASIC BOOKS
A Member of the Perseus Books Group
New York

Set in 11 point Sabon LT Standard by the Perseus Books Group

Books published by Basic Books are available at special discounts for bulk
purchases in the United States by corporations, institutions, and other
organizations. For more information, please contact the Special Markets
Department at the Perseus Books Group, 2300 Chestnut Street, Suite 200,
Philadelphia, PA 19103, or call (800) 810-4145, ext. 5000, or e-mail
special.markets@perseusbooks.com.

A CIP catalog record for this book is available from the Library of Congress.
ISBN: 978-0-465-06482-3
E-BOOK: 978-0-465-03994-4
Published in the UK by Allen Lane
ISBN: 978-0241004609

10 9 8 7 6 5 4 3 2 1

For Hugh

When thou hast reached La Haye, survey it well,
Here was the heat and centre of the strife;
This point must Britain hold whate'er befell,
And here both armies were profuse of life:
Once it was lost, . . and then a stander by
Belike had trembled for the victory.

Robert Southey,
'The Poet's Pilgrimage to Waterloo' (1816)

Contents

List of Maps		x
Acknowledgements		xi
Preface		xv
1	Prelude	1
2	For King and Fatherland	9
3	A Tragedy of Errors	21
4	Bolting the Barn Door	33
5	Inferno	55
6	Hand to Hand	77
7	'Heat and centre of the strife'	101
8	Legacy: A 'German Victory'?	111
	Appendices	129
	Bibliography	135
	Notes	147
	Index	175

Maps

1. La Haye Sainte   xviii
2. The Strategic Situation: Night of 17–18 June   xix
3. French and Allied Deployments May 1815   xx

Acknowledgements

My greatest debt is to my wife, Anita Bunyan, for organizing several visits to the battlefield, for commenting extensively on the text and for everything else.

This book began about forty years ago when my father, David Simms, first introduced me to the battle of Waterloo as a young boy; I remain extremely grateful to him, and to my mother, Anngret, for their encouragement. I was prompted to write it five years ago when I learned that my friend Nathalie Hamilton, née de Lannoy, knew well the farm of La Haye Sainte, whose owner had been a childhood friend. I thank her for bringing me together with him, Count François Cornet d'Elzius and his German wife, Suzanne. Both were extremely hospitable and helpful. They are mindful of the enormous historic importance of La Haye Sainte, but please bear in mind that it is their home and still a working farm. I ask readers to respect their privacy.

Acknowledgements

I have also been very fortunate to draw on the expertise of students, colleagues, friends and others, many of whom read and commented on earlier drafts of this book. Torsten Riotte's work on the origins of the King's German Legion provided me with very helpful background. Ilya Berkovich first made me aware of the importance of ideology in the combat motivation of old regime armies. Jasper Heinzen's work proved invaluable in understanding the complex Anglo-German legacy of the battle of Waterloo, and especially its Hanoverian dimension. My old friend James Carleton Paget read and greatly improved the text. Wiebke Meier, the translator of the German edition, spotted a number of mistakes and inconsistencies. So did my copy-editor, Bela Cunha.

I also thank Stella Child of the Bexhill Hanoverian Study Group, which has done so much to preserve the legacy of the King's German Legion in Britain. Barbara Hoffmann helped me with documents at the Hanoverian State Archives. Jamie Hood of the National Army Museum showed me how to use a Baker Rifle. Jens Mastnak and Michael-Andreas Tänzer of the Arbeitskreis Hannoversche Militärgeschichte corrected many mistakes and made many helpful suggestions, too many to be acknowledged individually. Jens Mastnak's forthcoming book on the Legion will be an indispensable resource on the subject and it is to be hoped that it quickly finds an English translator.

Acknowledgements

I am very grateful to them all. Needless to say, any remaining errors are my own.

My parents-in-law, Richard and Aileen Bunyan, not only hosted me during part of the writing of this book, but also put their capacious historical library at my disposal. My two daughters, Constance and Katherine, bore with my interest in the battle of Waterloo.

This book would not have been written without the support of the Carl Friedrich von Siemens Stiftung, Munich, which awarded me a one-year Fellowship during which this book was for the most part researched and written. I thank them through their director, Professor Heinrich Meier.

The Master and Fellows of Peterhouse provided, as ever, a stimulating and congenial environment for an historian. So did the Department of Politics and International Studies at the University of Cambridge. Hazel Dunn heroically printed out documents for me. Marcus von Salisch of the Military Historical Research Institute in Potsdam kindly arranged for a preliminary bibliography to be compiled and my association with that august institution has sharpened my understanding of military history no end.

Further thanks are due to Ronald Asch, Alessandro Barbero, Georg Baumann, Jacques Beauroy, Gemma Betros, John Bew, Tim Blanning, Martin Boycott Brown, Arndt Brendecke, Mike Broers, Jonathan Bronitsky, Etienne de Durand,

Acknowledgements

Charles Esdaile, Liam Fitzgerald, Dominik Geppert, Daniela Hacke, Mary Catherine Hart, Rona Hemingway, Leighton James, Linda von Keyserlinck, Shivan Mahendrajah, Rebecca Newell, Jochen Rudersdorf, Frederick Schofield, Adam Storring, Geoffrey Wawro, Hanna Weibye and Mark Wishon.

Finally, I thank my son Hugh, whose interest in the battle of Waterloo rekindled my own, and whose knowledge of the Napoleonic Wars already greatly exceeds that of his father. This book is for him.

Preface

Despite the passage of 200 years and the twentieth-century effusions of bloodshed on a scale previously unimaginable, the Battle of Waterloo has lost none of its resonance.[1] Countless towns, railway stations and monuments across the world are testament to its enduring importance. The concept of 'meeting one's Waterloo' has entered the English language, and was immortalized in the pop group Abba's Eurovision winner 'Waterloo', thanks to which a generation of teenagers knew – even if it was all they knew – that at 'Waterloo Napoleon did surrender'. Although the war did not end immediately, the battle was so conclusive that its name has become a byword for decisive victory.

'Waterloo,' Victor Hugo wrote, 'was not a battle but a change in the direction of the world.' Waterloo solved, as the historian Jeremy Black has argued, 'the Western Question', of whether Europe would be dominated by France or by a loose society of independent states, whose balance was guaranteed by Great Britain and her continental partners. This made the battle, as the British Chancellor of the Exchequer George Osborne recently suggested, half in jest and half as a swipe at his Labour predecessors, 'a great victory of coalition forces over a discredited former regime that had impoverished millions'.[2] Without the Prussian intervention in the battle, Ben Macintyre wrote in *The Times*, 'we'd all be speaking French'.[3]

Contemporaries, too, were in no doubt about the significance of the struggle. Napoleon's flight from exile in Elba in February 1815 plunged Europe back into war. Of course, it is likely that, whatever the outcome at Waterloo, the Russians and Austrians would ultimately have brought Napoleon to heel again. But nobody could be sure of that, which was why all eyes were on the allied army in Belgium. 'It is up to you to save the world,' Tsar Alexander of Russia told its commander, the Duke of Wellington, before he set out.[4] Shortly after the battle the poet Byron wrote in *Childe Harold* of Waterloo as a 'place of skulls' where the 'united nations' prevailed over the French tyrant.[5] This sense of 'united nations' was new. If Napoleon had once marshalled contingents from across the continent – so that at Leipzig in 1813 one could reasonably say that one half of Europe was battling the other – by Waterloo his force was almost entirely made up of Frenchmen. The allied army, by contrast, was thoroughly multinational, with even the British making up only a plurality of Wellington's men at Waterloo. Byron's image of the 'united nations' triumphing over tyranny proved so powerful to Winston Churchill and Franklin Delano Roosevelt that they borrowed it for a new structure of world governance which has remained with us to this day.

This drama has been told often and told well. One crucial aspect of the battle, however, has been relatively neglected: the epic defence of the farm of La Haye Sainte at the centre of the allied line by the men of the 2nd Light Battalion King's German Legion. Thanks to the availability of new sources, including unpublished material in the Hanoverian archives, we now know much more about these 400-odd riflemen. They were motivated by a combination of ideological opposition to Napoleonic tyranny, dynastic loyalty to the King of England, German patriotism, regimental camaraderie, personal bonds of friendship and professional ethos. These men, and their reinforcements, held off Napoleon for long enough to change the course of the battle. This is their story.

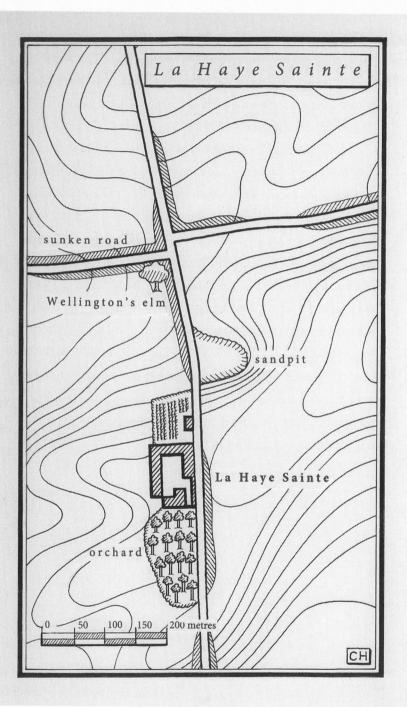

La Haye Sainte

sunken road

Wellington's elm

sandpit

La Haye Sainte

orchard

0   50   100   150   200 metres

CH

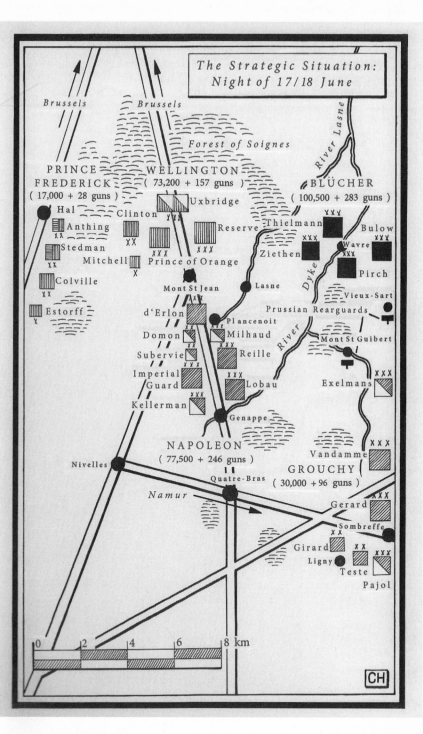

The Strategic Situation: Night of 17/18 June

Brussels
Brussels
Forest of Soignes
River Lasne

PRINCE
FREDERICK
(17,000 + 28 guns)

WELLINGTON
(73,200 + 157 guns)

BLÜCHER
(100,500 + 283 guns)

Hal
Anthing
Clinton
Uxbridge
Reserve
Thielmann
Bulow
Stedman
Mitchell
Prince of Orange
Ziethen
Wavre
Pirch
Colville
Mont St Jean
Lasne
Vieux-Sart
Estorff
d'Erlon
Plancenoit
Prussian Rearguards
Domon
Milhaud
Subervie
Reille
Mont St Guibert
Imperial
Guard
Lobau
Exelmans
Kellerman
Genappe
Nivelles
NAPOLEON
(77,500 + 246 guns)
Vandamme
GROUCHY
(30,000 + 96 guns)
Quatre-Bras
Namur
Gerard
Sombreffe
Girard
Ligny
Teste
Pajol

0   2   4   6   8 km

CH

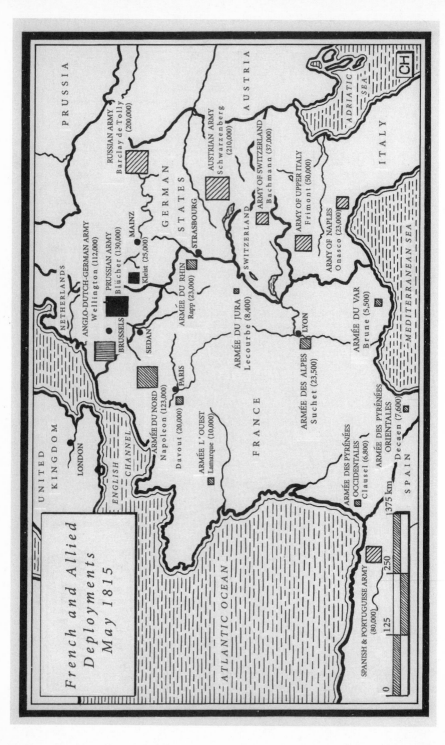

French and Allied Deployments May 1815

PRUSSIA

UNITED KINGDOM

NETHERLANDS

RUSSIAN ARMY
Barclay de Tolly (200,000)

ANGLO-DUTCH-GERMAN ARMY
Wellington (112,000)

PRUSSIAN ARMY
Blücher (130,000)

MAINZ
Kleist (25,000)

GERMAN STATES

AUSTRIA

AUSTRIAN ARMY
Schwarzenberg (210,000)

ARMY OF SWITZERLAND
Bachmann (37,000)

ITALY

ADRIATIC SEA

BRUSSELS

STRASBOURG

SEDAN

ARMÉE DU RHIN
Rapp (23,000)

SWITZERLAND

ARMY OF UPPER ITALY
Frimont (50,000)

ARMY OF NAPLES
Onasco (23,000)

LONDON

ENGLISH CHANNEL

ARMÉE DU NORD
Napoléon (123,000)

PARIS

Davout (20,000)

ARMÉE DU JURA
Lecourbe (8,400)

LYON

ARMÉE DU VAR
Brune (5,500)

ARMÉE L'OUEST
Lamarque (10,000)

FRANCE

ARMÉE DES ALPES
Suchet (23,500)

MEDITERRANEAN SEA

ATLANTIC OCEAN

ARMÉE DES PYRÉNÉES
OCCIDENTALES
Clausel (6,800)

ARMÉE DES PYRÉNÉES
ORIENTALES
Decaen (7,600)

SPAIN

SPANISH & PORTUGUESE ARMY
(80,000)

0   125   250   375 km

CH

1
Prelude

Belgium, early afternoon, Saturday 17 June 1815. The French have worsted Marshal Blücher's Prussians at Ligny and the Duke of Wellington's allied army at the crossroads of Quatre Bras the day before. Now Napoleon is making haste to destroy Wellington's retreating army before he can unite with Blücher.

Mercifully, the riflemen of the 2nd Light Battalion of the King's German Legion had missed the battle at Quatre Bras the day before,[1] but they witnessed its appalling aftermath: 'a horrible field of corpses ... literally swimming in blood, which at every step went over our ankles', in the words of Rifleman Friedrich Lindau.[2] The general feeling, as Lieutenant Emanuel Biedermann recalled, was that Napoleon had caught the allied army napping;[3] contrary to myth, however, none of the brigade officers were still in the clothes they had worn to the Duchess of Richmond's ball in Brussels a few days earlier.[4] At around 2 p.m., the 2nd Light Battalion was detailed to relieve the skirmishers holding off the pursuing French and withdraw. Together with their fellow riflemen of the British 95th Regiment,[5] they formed the rearguard for the entire allied army. Starving and exhausted, the Germans rested in a meadow near Genappe. Despite the fact that they were told to prepare for a French attack, most of the men promptly fell asleep. They were soon woken, however, by a sudden thunderstorm and downpour. Then a detachment of Brunswick Hussars galloped up and told them they must withdraw immediately, as the enemy was already encroaching on all sides. The Germans now retreated at the double through sunken roads, which the rain had turned into streams, and muddy cornfields, towards the military road which led to Brussels.[6] Once past Genappe – where 'the water reached to their knees'[7] – the battalion was ordered to keep the highway free for the retreating allied cavalry and artillery. The riflemen continued to march in the fields on either side of the road, through high corn and soil soft from the downpour.

As they trudged northwards, the Germans pressed together more closely in order to minimize their exposure to the driving rain. Against the leaden skies and the thunder and lightning of the elements, the flash and crash of artillery continued to light up the horizon and reverberate across the fields. At regular intervals, allied horsemen charged past them in order to drive off the encroaching French cavalry and skirmishers. By the end of the day, the riders were so soiled that the riflemen could no longer tell from their uniforms whether they were friend or foe. At times, the French advanced within a few hundred paces of the Germans. On more than one occasion, the battalion was forced to halt and deploy in square, the sides bristling with their distinctive sword bayonets, in order to deter enemy cavalry. They would have been surprised to read Wellington's later dispatch to the effect that the enemy had not 'attempt[ed] to molest our march to the rear' after Quatre Bras.[8]

The Germans were still better off than the unfortunate Belgian civilians who were attempting to escape the advancing French. Lieutenant Biedermann pitied the 'men [who were] driving their cattle before them, others bearing bundles, women carrying or pulling their children after them, [all] fleeing moaning and weeping'.[9]

It was about half past seven in the evening of Saturday 17 June when the first riflemen reached the heights of Mont-Saint-Jean near the village of Waterloo. By the time the last Legionnaires arrived it was dark, though the night sky was occasionally illuminated by muzzle flashes and the air was punctuated by gunfire and shouted orders as the retreating columns were marshalled at the crossroads just beyond the substantial farmhouse of La Haye Sainte, which stood adjacent to the Brussels–Charleroi road, named – accounts differ – either after the crown of thorns worn by Christ at his crucifixion or, more prosaically, after a brambled hedge which enclosed a nearby meadow.[10] It was later still when the 400 or so Germans received word that they were to occupy the farm.[11] The retreat was over.

La Haye Sainte, the farm in which the 2nd Light Battalion was to fight its most celebrated action, consisted of a stable, a piggery, a barn, a substantial farmhouse, a low wall and a pond, arranged around a large courtyard. It was a common enough type of dwelling for the area. The farmer and his family had fled. The house was large, with walls in places more than a metre thick, and high ceilings. There were large dormer windows on the first storey, and hay and straw in the floor above, which had no windows. A passage led through the stable to the fields on the western side; the main gate and a wicket gate gave access to the road to the east. A passage and two doors opened on to the kitchen garden immediately north of the house. Its northern and western sides were surrounded by a hedge and the eastern side, which gave on to the road, by a wall; the garden contained a well and an outhouse. Just to the south of the main buildings was a large orchard, three sides of which were enclosed by another hedge, and the fourth by a large barn (about thirty metres long) and a low wall, through which a gate led into the courtyard. The buildings themselves were undamaged, but because La Haye Sainte lay just beside the main allied line of withdrawal, it had already been plundered by passing soldiers. Most importantly, they had torn down the barn door opening on to the field to the left to provide firewood for some of the thousands of miserable men camped in the countryside around. Captain Jonathan Leach of the 95th Rifles just across the road describes sleeping on ground so boggy that it resembled 'a snipe marsh'. Rifleman Simon Lehmann of the 1st Light Battalion, who spent the night in the sunken road behind the farm, must also have been extremely uncomfortable.[12]

Unfortunately for the Germans, most of the hay in the outbuildings was also carried away. The animals, however, were slaughtered and the meat was shared with the neighbouring line battalion of the Legion; the riflemen overlooked the calf in the piggery, however.[13] The men showed little interest in the food: for the moment, the main priority was to stay, or to get, dry. The lucky ones were able to take shelter within the buildings. Private Friedrich Lindau was one of those who drew the short straw. His company was sent to the orchard, where there was virtually no protection from the elements and where they were so close to the enemy that the soldiers were forbidden to light a fire. Lindau did, however, succeed in making off with a pocketful of peas he found in the farmhouse.

Most of the riflemen, though, had fallen into a stupor, their senses numbed by tiredness, hunger and the incessant rain. Rather than lie in the damp they leant against walls and trees, or sat on their knapsacks, staring vacantly into space. Even outside the main buildings, few tried to light a fire – admittedly no easy matter in the downpour – or to cook the fresh meat they had been issued. Instead, they warmed themselves with alcohol. The enterprising Lindau sneaked into the cellar and made off with a canteen of wine, which he shared with his comrades and with soldiers of the 1st Light Battalion stationed nearby. It was not long before Germans who had bivouacked further away, such as Corporal Meyer of the Bremen Field Battalion, came to scrounge some drink as well. Repeated return trips to the cellar ensured that the men in the orchard, and probably much of the rest of the garrison, were well supplied with alcohol. Eventually, Lindau lay down for the night at the far end of the orchard facing the enemy, his rifle at the ready. Lieutenant Emanuel Biedermann, who was also trying to sleep among the trees, recalls that now 'quiet and a deep peace followed the racket of the day'.[14]

On the other side of the valley, the pursuing French also settled in for the night. Many of them were Napoleonic veterans of many years' standing, others young recruits.[15] Their personal loyalty to the emperor was often fervent. Two days before the battle, the advancing columns observed 'a young soldier or rather a trunk of a man' who had 'two legs taken off by a cannon ball', as well as severe face and chest wounds which had not yet healed. On seeing his comrades, the unfortunate lifted his hands and called out: 'Long live the emperor. I have lost my two legs, but I don't care. Victory is ours. Long live the emperor.'[16] Like their German counterparts the French spent the afternoon and night of 17 June in the rain around spluttering campfires. 'The night was terrible,' the French commander opposite La Haye Sainte recalls; 'rain fell in abundance', which made 'the manoeuvring of artillery very difficult. The men had spent the night without shelter and nobody had been able to make a fire.'[17] It was too wet to cook, so men like Corporal Canler of the 28th Line Regiment held on to the sheep they had captured nearby and the small square of butter he had picked up the day before.[18] He and his comrades were part of Bourgeois's 2nd Brigade on Alix's 1st Division, one of four in d'Erlon's 1st Corps. Like the Germans in La Haye Sainte, d'Erlon's men had taken no part in the fighting at Quatre Bras, having wasted the day marching fruitlessly back and forth due to contradictory orders. After being reproached by Napoleon – as he recalled – 'in a very chagrined tone', d'Erlon was determined not to be found wanting again.[19]

As they bedded down for the night, the riflemen at La Haye Sainte knew that there would probably be a major engagement once the French main force arrived. Lieutenant Biedermann remembers seeing many of the men deep in thought that night. 'I too wondered,' he writes, 'whether I would see my homeland and my dear ones again or whether an enemy sword would propel me out of my unsettled life . . . At the threshold of death, the past and the future appear in a much more serious light than otherwise.'[20] Neither Biedermann, Lindau nor the rest of the battalion, however, could have foreseen just how severely they would be tested the following day.

2

For King and Fatherland

The Germans of the 2nd Light Battalion had come a long way.[1] They were not just in La Haye Sainte 'because they were there'. Their road to Waterloo began twelve years before, in 1803, when their Hanoverian homeland in northern Germany was overrun by Napoleon.[2] Many had entered the new 'King's German Legion' (KGL) established by their ruler, George III of England, who was also Elector of Hanover, towards the end of that year. Others joined later to escape the rigours of the French occupation, travelling from Hamburg via Husum and Heligoland, or via Barth near Stralsund in Swedish Pomerania.[3] The two rifle units – the 1st and the 2nd Light Battalions – were the very first to be established; line, artillery and cavalry formations followed later as more and more recruits arrived in Britain from the continent. The flow slowed to a trickle in 1809–10, as the occupation authorities clamped down, and in 1811–12 several Hanoverians were executed by the French for recruiting for the Legion. It was envisaged that many different nationalities would enlist in the Legion. In 1811, the British War Office laid down that the Legion should recruit 'none but such as are Natives of Germany and speak, or at least understand, German, including all German countries, which are now incorporated with France, likewise the possessions of the House of Austria and those which belonged formerly to Russia and Holland'; the enlistment of 'French, Italians, Danes, Swedes, Russians, Spaniards or Portuguese' was explicitly ruled out.[4]

At Waterloo, the line battalions were the most mixed, with about 50 per cent of the rank and file coming from German territories other than Hanover, especially Prussia, and – despite the War Office's injunctions – even Russia and Denmark. Generally speaking, the proportion of Hanoverians in the Light Battalions was higher, making them more homogeneous and very likely also more cohesive. All the same, about one-third of the men in La Haye Sainte hailed from Prussia, Bavaria and other parts of the old Holy Roman Empire, and there were even Poles (such as Alexander Dobritzky of the 3rd Company) and Flemings (such as Baptist Charrier of the 5th Company).[5] Wherever they came from, the men who enlisted in the 2nd Light

Battalion had embarked on an odyssey leading from Hanover, via the Legion's English base camp at Bexhill on the Channel Coast, expeditions to Northern Germany and garrison duty in Ireland, in 1805–6, to the Baltic in 1807–8, the Iberian Peninsula in 1808–9, to the Scheldt in 1809, back to the Peninsula in 1811–13, through Southern France, and the shadow of demobilization after Napoleon's exile to Elba, to the slopes of Mont Saint Jean in Belgium.

Unlike most of the foreign formations which fought in the coalitions against Napoleon, the King's German Legion was part of the British regular army. For those not already in royal service, commissions were temporary until August 1810 and were then made permanent by Act of Parliament in recognition of the Legion's services in the Peninsula. Some of its officers were British, especially in the 2nd Light Battalion,[6] as were the paymasters; its bankers were the London firm of Greenword, Cox and Company in Craig's Court off Whitehall (eventually absorbed into Lloyds bank).[7] The language of command was generally English, as was the rank structure; the men of the 2nd Light Battalion were equipped with standard-issue Baker rifles, and they wore the same distinctive green jackets as the British riflemen.[8] If they enlisted in Britain, recruits were paid the same bounty as the King's other subjects. They swore the same oath, and were – as the official proclamation put it – generally 'subject to the same regulations and articles of war as his majesty's British troops'.[9] The Legion adopted the English enthusiasm for physical exercise, such as rowing, wrestling, stick-fencing and boxing, and team sports such as football and cricket.[10] The officers could avail themselves of a progressive military education, and were allowed to attend artillery courses in arithmetic, drawing, geometry, geography and fortifications.[11] The Germans never served as a single corps, but were always brigaded with other British units on operations, though at Waterloo their divisional commander, Sir Charles von Alten, was a Hanoverian.[12] By Waterloo the Legion had more than a decade of combat experience fighting alongside the rest of Wellington's army.[13] Of a total of some 30,000 Legionnaires who served throughout the conflict, about 1,300 were killed in action, with nearly 5,900 dying from all causes.

The two light battalions were unusual within the Legion in that they never completely adopted British drill regulations, or the English language.[14] German remained in use throughout the 2nd Light Battalion, but English was prescribed for sentry duty, where it was vital to avoid misunderstandings, and on parade. Majors and adjutants were chosen with their knowledge of English in mind. Many of the officers were already fluent. Those who were not took private lessons, often with female tutors, in which they made great strides. Some officers who had begun their diaries in German completed them in English.[15] They often switched between the two languages in conversation and correspondence. For example, a table on losses and additions to the fighting strength has entries under 'joined' and 'total effectives' as well as *'gestorben'* ('died') and *'verabschiedet ohne Pension'* ('discharged without a pension').[16] Some senior officers, such as General von Alten, who commanded the light division in Spain, and Sir Julius von Hartmann,[17] re-invented themselves as hybrid Anglo-German gentlemen, affecting the manners and dress of their hosts. It was also common for the rank and file to adopt – or to be given – English first names: one list has a John Hennes, a Frederick Almutz and a Henry Ebeling, as well as the more German Wilhelm Witz.[18] So by Waterloo, even the 'German' 2nd Light Battalion of the King's German Legion had effectively become bilingual. We would nowadays describe it as an agent of 'cultural transfer'.

The eighteenth-century forebears of the Hanoverians, the auxiliary regiments deployed in England during the French invasion scares of the Seven Years War, had been despised as agents of royal despotism.[19] These sentiments had attenuated but by no means evaporated by the Revolutionary and Napoleonic period.[20] The radical William Cobbett was imprisoned as late as 1810 in the aftermath of his diatribes against the King's German Legion. For this reason, the King's German Legion was regarded with some trepidation when it marched to its depot at Bexhill on the south coast of England, camping on the village commons en route. When two officers passed a couple of farmers on the way to the pub, they overheard the following conversation. 'Where are you going, Jack?' one asked. 'We are going to the common to see the wild Germans,' the other answered.[21] Upon their return to the camp they found the men eating, observed by astonished locals. 'Look at them,' the locals cried, 'they have spoons, knives and forks like ourselves.' Soon, however, the Legion was accepted at all levels of English society. Their strong musical traditions, in particular, made an impression on the population. Many of the officers and rank and file married local girls.[22] One of them was Captain Philip Holtzermann of the 1st Light Battalion, later posted just beside La Haye Sainte, who wed Mary-Ann Pumphrey, daughter of the customs officer at Bexhill, in 1812. Others were Rifleman Henry Bush (or Busch as he was baptized), of the 2nd Light Battalion, who married Harriet Haselden in September 1810, and Rifleman George (Gottfried) Heinz, also of the 2nd Light Battalion, who married local girl Mary Anne Burt in January 1813.[23] Even today, the streetscape of Bexhill-on-Sea, as it is now called, records the connection: the barracks and the Germans are long gone, but there is still a 'Barrack Road', a 'Hanover Close' nearby and a 'Hanover House' on the old High Street.

The Legion had a distinctive ethos. Relations between officers and men were closer than in most British formations: the general tone in the memoir literature is respectful and affectionate on both sides. This also seems to have applied to officers of British origin, perhaps because they tended to be men from less 'smart' backgrounds who could not afford or obtain a commission in one of the more prestigious English or Scottish regiments. Indeed, the Legion was unusual in that commissions could not be bought. Moreover, many men of the King's German Legion, far from being mere continental mercenaries in the King's pay, perceived themselves as ideological warriors against Napoleon and French domination generally.[24] They pointedly refused to join the French-sponsored 'Hanoverian Legion', which would have been a much more convenient choice of career.[25] The 2nd Light Battalion certainly expressed none of the grudging admiration for 'Boney' which one often found in British ranks, or the ideological sympathies for the Napoleonic project frequently expressed by other Germans, for example in the Rhineland. Likewise, the rank and file perceived themselves not as the 'scum of the earth', for whom military service was simply an escape from poverty or incarceration, nor simply as honest military professionals for whom service was a life-long occupation, but as free Germans and loyal subjects of the Elector-King, who had volunteered to rid their land of the French scourge. In this, they resembled the 'Free French' of General de Gaulle during the Second World War.[26]

Thus Julius von Hartmann refused to collaborate with the French and condemned the 'fearfulness and lack of character' of those who did so.[27] Friedrich Heinecke, who recruited for the Legion in North Germany, spoke of the 'patriotic sentiment' of the men, their 'mighty bitterness against the hereditary enemy', and their determination to 'fight against Napoleon and to cast off the yoke of French tyranny'.[28] One surgeon of the Legion wrote of leaving his native town of Minden 'in order to breathe more freely in free England, and to provide myself with a future while my prospects at home were obscured by a sinister veil'.[29] Such sentiments were shared by ordinary soldiers such as Rifleman Friedrich Lindau of the 2nd Light Battalion, who spoke of his 'implacable resentment against France and the French'.[30] This patriotism applied not only to the Hanoverians but to the other Germans as well. Even the Swiss Emanuel Biedermann, a lieutenant in the 2nd Light Battalion, spoke of his desire to 'drive out the French who had no respect for any international law' and looked forward to 'we Germans and Swiss [having] an active role in the wars of liberation on the soil of the Fatherland'.[31] These feelings chimed with those of the Legion's British officers. Whatever his private reservations against 'these heavy selfish Germans', Lieutenant Edmund Wheatley of the 5th Line Battalion noted that they were all at Waterloo 'to deal out thunder and confusion to the opposers of the English constitution'.[32] The King's German Legion, in short, was an Anglo-German hybrid designed to tap into the human resources of the old Holy Roman Empire in order to expel the French, and to restore German liberty and the European balance of power.[33]

The Legionnaires were a socially diverse group, even among the officers. Georg Hartog Gerson, who joined the Legion as a hospital assistant, came from a long line of Jewish doctors in Altona near Hamburg. His grandfather had been in charge of the Jewish hospital there, and his father and elder brothers were medical doctors as well. He studied at Berlin and the Hanoverian university of Göttingen, securing a medical doctorate in April 1810. A year later, not long after entering the Legion, Gerson was commissioned as assistant surgeon to the 5th Line Battalion of the King's German Legion. He served in the Peninsula and Southern France. In June 1815, his regiment formed part of the 2nd King's German Legion Infantry Brigade, commanded by the legendary Christian von Ompteda.[34]

Indeed, the Omptedas epitomized the Hanoverian struggle against Napoleon. Christian Friedrich von Ompteda was a major in the Hanoverian Guards Regiment when his country was overrun by the French in 1803. He joined the Legion as soon as it was formed and served in Northern Germany, and against the Danes in 1807, enduring a brief period of captivity after being shipwrecked off the Dutch coast. Taking command of the 1st Light Battalion in October 1812, Ompteda fought with distinction in the Peninsula and Southern France. Despite a tendency towards excitability and nervous disorder, which periodically forced him to take extraordinary leave, he became commander of the 2nd King's German Legion Brigade. His younger brother, Ludwig Karl Georg von Ompteda, served as a Hanoverian envoy, tirelessly fighting Napoleon on the diplomatic front.[35] During the Waterloo campaign he was ambassador to Prussia, whose forces were hastening to Wellington's aid in Belgium. The wars against Napoleon had already claimed a heavy price from the family. Their cousin Captain Ferdinand von Ompteda fell ill on active service and died in October 1809 at Egham near Windsor. Another cousin, Captain August von Ompteda, was killed in action at Elvas, Portugal, in April 1811.

Just before setting out on the Waterloo campaign, Christian learned that his much-loved third brother, Ferdinand, a fellow officer in the Legion, had died after a short illness.[36] 'My dear Ludwig,' he wrote to his surviving brother, 'the [three-cornered] clover-leaf [the family emblem] held for half a century.' Christian recalled 'Ferdinand's quiet sensibility, [and Ludwig's] skilful handling of differences arising from fate and my own unstable temperament', which had sustained the brothers through thick and thin. Now that Ferdinand was lost, he enjoined Ludwig that they should 'tie their bonds closer and tighter than ever and not allow the autumn of their lives to rob the leaves of their family symbol of its living freshness'. The sight of the three-sided clover, Christian felt, would be a 'constant reminder of our loss'.[37] In practical terms, he was anxious about the future of his dead brother's sons, the two eldest of whom were serving 'for the interim' with the 5th Line Battalion. Christian believed that they were 'good, and full of good will' but too young to fight; the youngest was only fourteen. Their safety was to be a pre-occupation for him in the days ahead. Ompteda looked forward to the fight with confidence, however, as he would be serving in the division of his 'old friend' Charles von Alten, with whom 'fate' had 'brought him together again'.[38]

The men in La Haye Sainte formed part of Ompteda's 2nd King's German Brigade. Usually, the 2nd Light Battalion was commanded by Lieutenant-Colonel David Martin. He was, however, absent at Waterloo. His place was taken by Major George Baring. The youngest son of a Hanoverian administrator, he spent most of his childhood engaged in various forms of rebellion and trying to avoid the private tuition arranged by his father. When Baring turned twelve, he decided to become a soldier. His father agreed, on condition that he join the infantry because he could not afford to equip his son for a cavalry regiment. Service in the Hanoverian army did not put an end to Baring's japes, however, not all of them very amusing from a present-day perspective. These included a prank against 'an elderly Jewess who had not wanted to lend money',[39] who was buried under a pile of planks heaped against her door. He was involved in a number of 'affairs of honour' over women, in the first of which he sustained a sword injury to an arm. In a later duel Baring disfigured an unfortunate antagonist – the once-handsome ensign von Dachsenhausen – by slashing him 'from the ear to the mouth'.[40] He received his baptism of fire in September 1793, against the French Revolutionary armies in Flanders, and was so badly wounded that he was initially given up for dead: an enemy bullet ploughed through his mouth and cheek, knocking out four of his teeth; pus continued to pour through his nose and ears for years afterwards.

Despite this experience, Baring returned to service as soon as he recovered. The Hanoverian collapse of 1803 left him adrift. Like many he felt that he 'could not stay among the French'; moreover, after sixteen years in the army, he 'now had and was nothing'. It was time for a radical decision, so Baring became involved in recruiting for the King's German Legion and soon joined it himself. He fought in North Germany, the Baltic, Walcheren, the Iberian Peninsula and Southern France. In May 1811, Baring particularly distinguished himself in Spain, where he suffered a minor injury during the brutal struggle for the village of Albuera. He served as aide de camp to Charles von Alten in the Peninsula, and appears to have been somewhat in awe of him. Later Baring was made a major in the 2nd Light Battalion. He seems to have been liked and respected by his men, who had already followed him into battle and possible death or injury on many previous occasions. Their loyalty, however, was about to receive its hardest test yet.

3

A Tragedy of Errors

The Duke of Wellington – who was informed in the early hours of 18 June that the Prussians would come to his aid later that day – decided to give battle. He knew the ground well, having reconnoitred it recently. Although Wellington would have preferred to fight at Rossomme further south, the heights of Mont-Saint-Jean, where Quartermaster de Lancey had halted the retreat, was also an excellent defensive position. It was bounded on both sides by fortifiable buildings; the slopes themselves allowed him to conceal his infantry well and provided a good field of fire. At 6 a.m. the Duke left his headquarters at Waterloo and headed for the battlefield. An hour later, Wellington embarked on an inspection of the allied position.[1] Anxious to prevent

Napoleon from cutting him off from the sea, he posted a large detachment further west at Hal; these 18,000 men or so took no further part in operations. On the battlefield itself, he sent the elite Guards Brigade and some Nassauers to the modest château of Hougoumont and its environs on his right (western) flank; he was so concerned to hold this position that additional engineering units, including those of the King's German Legion, were dispatched to fortify the buildings. His left (eastern) flank rested on the villages of La Haye and Papelotte. In the centre, the Duke posted Bylandt's inexperienced Dutch–Belgian brigade on the forward slope just to the east of La Haye Sainte. Most of the rest of the army was deployed on the reverse slopes along the ridge, on both sides of the farmhouse, with the weaker elements to the left closest to where the Prussian relief column was expected.

The allied centre, the vital area around the crossroads and La Haye Sainte, was assigned to the 3rd British Infantry Division under the command of General Charles von Alten, and in particular to Ompteda's 2nd King's German Legion Brigade. Most of them had not fought at Quatre Bras and were thus relatively fresh. The 1st Light (Rifle) Battalion of the King's German Legion, commanded by Lieutenant-Colonel Louis von dem Busche, was placed immediately to the right of the crossroads. One of their number was the recently married Captain Philip Holtzermann. Behind them lay Lieutenant-Colonel von Schröder's 8th

Line Battalion of the Legion. To their right was the Legion's 5th Line Battalion, under Lieutenant-Colonel von Linsingen. Just beyond them lay the Lüneburg Light Battalion of the Hanoverian army, which had been reconstituted after Napoleon's defeat in 1813–14. The area between La Haye Sainte and Hougoumont was screened by skirmishers, including many from the 1st Light Battalion of the Legion. Baring's 2nd Light Battalion would hold La Haye Sainte itself, a routine deployment because light infantry were considered best for built-up areas, hand-to-hand combat and indeed any role which was not strictly defined in the standard manuals.

Neither Wellington nor the corps commander, the Prince of Orange, nor the divisional commander, von Alten, seem to have given the farmhouse any great thought. Instead, the Legion's engineers were sent, with all their tools, to Hougoumont. This was a surprising move, because possession of the buildings was critical to the defence of the crossroads and thus of the whole allied centre. Witnesses recall that the brigade commander, Ompteda, was 'deeply dissatisfied by the defensive preparations made by the corps command, especially by the absence of any artillery'[2] in La Haye Sainte. He spent part of the night in conclave with Baring, Lieutenant-Colonel von dem Busche of the 1st Light Battalion, the brigade adjutant, Major von Einem, and his personal aide de camp, Captain von Brandis, in a room in the farmhouse,[3] beside a blazing fire and over a cup of hot soup. It must have been then that the decision was taken to fortify the place as much as possible. This was going to be a difficult task, because the Legion's engineers were earmarked for Hougoumont. Forsaking the warmth of the farmhouse, Ompteda spent the rest of the night around the staff watch fire of the 5th Line Battalion, a lonely and brooding figure. He refused all offers of a woollen blanket to protect him from the elements, because the rank and file had strict orders from above not to use theirs, presumably so that they could react quickly in the event of a French surprise attack during the night. It was characteristic of the man that he would not ask his men to do anything that he was not prepared to do himself.

At dawn on 18 June, Lindau was woken by Rifleman Harz, who demanded more wine. It was still raining heavily. 'Today is going to be a tough day,' he said, 'and I am going to die because I dreamed quite definitely that I would get a bullet through my body that did me no misfortune and that I slept contented.' The farmhouse had become a hive of activity. It had stopped raining, and the garrison had cast off its lethargy of the night before. Some of the men were put to cooking a pig, which,[4] as Lieutenant Biedermann recalls, was slaughtered with more speed than skill. Hunger, the officer noted wryly, was not conducive to 'fraternity', because he himself received no meat, but only a few peas and some salt.[5] Others, despite the absence of suitable tools, knocked loopholes in the courtyard walls and erected a makeshift firing platform to enable the other defenders to fire over them. Strenuous, but inadequate, efforts were made to block the gap left by the removal of the barn door. The banging and hammering must have made further sleep for the rest of the garrison impossible. Given that his canteen was now empty of wine, Lindau suggested to Harz that they warm themselves by helping the neighbouring British riflemen from the 95th Regiment to construct a barricade across the Brussels road, flush with the south-facing court-yard wall.[6] Most of the farm equipment which had not been burned in the night was now piled up in the road: half a wagon, various farm implements, ladders and three spiked French cannon; the obstacle was bolstered with several tree trunks and foliage cut down nearby.[7] Later, Wellington's aide Lord Cathcart remarked that 'it was not much' of an obstacle 'at any time',[8] and it was so flimsy that a party of friendly Dragoons simply rode through it during the morning, forcing the long-suffering detail to rebuild it.[9] For the British and German riflemen holding the road, however, it was better than nothing.

All across the allied line, the men stood to arms. The mental and physical state of the Legionnaires in light of the previous day's downpour, their lack of sleep and the prospect of murderous battle against a seasoned foe can only be guessed at. Many of them must have been hungry, shivering, coughing, with running noses and blocked noses and ears; some will have been too excited to eat properly.[10] The sun burst through at around 8 a.m., which brought some relief. The air erupted to the sound of weapons being cleaned and fired in order to establish whether they were still working after the rain of the day and night before. Women camp-followers were sent away to the rear on the Duke's orders.[11] In the 5th Line Battalion of the KGL, Lieutenant Wheatley watched the French manoeuvre on the opposing slopes. 'We could perceive,' he writes, 'shoals of . . . gloomy bodies glid[ing] down, disjointing then contracting, like fields of animated clods sweeping over the plains, like melted lava from a Volcano, boding ruin and destruction to whatever dared impede its course. It had a fairy look and bordered on the supernatural in appearance.' At this moment, the assistant regimental surgeon, Georg Gerson, tapped him on the shoulder and remarked, 'That's a battle, my boy! That's something like preparation,' before adding as a two-edged parting shot that he was off to the hospital and 'hope[d] to see you there'.[12]

Baring had six under-strength companies – a total of 378 effectives.[13] He had three senior officers: the second-in-command, acting-Major Bösewiel, as well as Captains Holtzermann and Schaumann. There were eleven lieutenants: Kiesler, Georg Meyer, Christian Meyer, Lindam, Riefkugel, Tobin, de Marweden, Carey, Biedermann, Graeme and one whose name could not be deciphered. Below them came the five ensigns: Frank, Smith, Baring, the teenage von Robertson and Timmann, the adjutant. They were assisted by twenty-four sergeants and fourteen buglers. Three medics – surgeon Heise, and his two assistants, Müller and Gehse – were there to look after the wounded. The rank and file comprised 317 corporals and ordinary riflemen. If he made an eve-of-battle speech to his men, it is not recorded. All we know is that, probably following his own instructions, which have not survived, he told his officers to fight as long as they could, and then withdraw to the main position.

Baring stationed one company, about eighty men, in the kitchen garden, under Lieutenant Georg Meyer, to prevent the farm from being surrounded, and in order to maintain communication with the main position on the ridge; surgeon Heise and his two assistants set up their casualty station there in the shed. Two companies under Lieutenants Tobin and Graeme were deployed in and around the courtyard, where they took up positions along the wall, in the dormer windows of the house and behind the barricade outside. Baring himself led three companies, about half the force, into the orchard facing the enemy.

His situation was highly precarious. The farm was well to the front of the allied line, with only two companies of the 1st Light Battalion, under Major von dem Busche,[14] and two companies of Hanoverian *Feldjäger* (light infantry), commanded by Major Spörcken, spread out in skirmish order before him. To Baring's left lay two guns on the road and two experienced companies of the 95th Rifle Regiment in a sandpit on the far side. The bulk of the allied infantry was at least 400 metres back, nearest being Lieutenant-General Thomas Picton's 5th British Infantry Division. The surrounding countryside – smooth and undulating today – was then broken up by gulleys in which enemy cavalry and skirmishers could lurk. Nor did Baring's riflemen enjoy a free field of fire. Despite all their efforts, the Legionnaires were able to create only a handful of new firing positions in the buildings, while a rise in the ground just below the orchard blocked their vision of the French lines to the south. Surprisingly, neither Baring nor his superiors seem to have made adequate provision for the resupply of ammunition, either by laying in a reserve within the farm, or having one nearby. This may have been because the two light battalions had had just one ammunition supply cart between them, and that had overturned into a ditch on the Brussels road during the headlong retreat.[15] As a result, Baring's battalion began the engagement with the standard issue of only sixty rounds apiece, which had to suffice for the entire action. Whatever the reason, and whoever was responsible, it was a blunder for which the Legionnaires would pay a heavy price in the afternoon.

The French spent the morning in much the same way. At dawn, Corporal Canler recalls, 'every company took down their muskets in order to grease them, changed their clothes and dried their bonnets.' Even very senior officers, such as Marshal d'Erlon's artillery commander Desales, had spent the night in the open, and were consequently drenched to the skin. On rising, Desales looked for and found a quiet place to change his clothes among the assorted wagons and coaches distributed across the French camp.[16] His forty-plus cannon would wreak havoc on the allied centre that day. Meanwhile, the private soldiers were feeding themselves. 'One of our corporals,' Canler recalls, 'who was something of a butcher's boy, killed, skinned, and cut into little pieces our poor little lamb.' The sheep was then cooked in butter: 'After an hour the captain and the lieutenant of the company came to take part in our meal, which I hasten to add, tasted awful because instead of the salt we lacked, our cook had put a handful of [gun-] powder into the pot.'[17]

Despite their miserable night, the shortage of food and the prospect of a hard fight ahead, morale among the men facing La Haye Sainte was high. When Napoleon passed by the 28th Line Regiment in the morning he was greeted 'by a spontaneous movement which resembled an electric convulsion: helmets, shakos, caps were born up on sabres and bayonets, with frenetic cries of "Long live the emperor"'.[18] The emperor spent the night in a farm at Le Caillou, about six and a half kilometres to the south of the allied position. To his intense relief, he found in the morning that Wellington had not slipped away under the cover of darkness, but was obviously preparing to give battle on the slopes of Mont-Saint-Jean. Napoleon spent the early morning indoors contemplating the rain and the continued arrival of more of his army. His orderly, General Gourgaud, informed him that the ground was too wet to permit an immediate attack. The emperor then reconnoitred the battlefield on horseback, advancing, as he recalled, as far as his 'skirmishers opposite La Haye Sainte'.[19] Obviously concerned about the situation there, Napoleon sent the engineering officer General Haxo to investigate the allied centre. He reported – correctly – that there were no signs of *field* fortifications; he may not have taken in the frantic and rather ineffectual attempts to fortify the farmhouse.[20] Napoleon was not overly worried about the Prussians, whom he believed to be in precipitate retreat eastwards, closely pursued by a large force under Marshal Grouchy. He was anxious, though, that the Duke might still elude him. For this reason Napoleon could not waste much time on manoeuvres, for example by outflanking the allied army to the west. Instead, he planned to grapple with Wellington through a frontal assault. He had about 74,000 men at his disposal, slightly more than the 68,000 in Wellington's army, and on average of higher quality.

At eleven in the morning, Napoleon dictated his orders to Marshal Ney, who was to direct the principal French attack in the middle of the battlefield.[21] The emperor did not work out a detailed plan because he did not yet know the exact disposition of the allied army. He therefore planned to begin with a probing attack by Reille's 2nd Corps on Wellington's right at Hougoumont, designed to tie down his men there, and force the Duke to commit some of his reserves. This would be followed by the main effort: a direct assault on the allied centre by d'Erlon's 1st Corps, beginning on the left and unfolding along the slope of Mont-Saint-Jean to the right. Once Wellington had shown the rest of his hand, the emperor planned to commit his own reserves, including the Imperial Guard if necessary. Napoleon's expectation was that once the main battle had been joined, the superior manoeuvring skill of his troops would win the day over his more cumbersome opponents.[22] That strategy, however, depended on forcing the enemy out of their well-established positions on the heights and in the fortified farmhouse.

The main focus of the French plan was thus the allied centre, and in particular its cornerstone, the farmhouse of La Haye Sainte. It is not clear whether Napoleon knew the buildings by that name,[23] but of their importance to him there can be no doubt. The emperor's instructions called for the capture of the 'village of Mont St Jean [*sic*] in order to seize the crossroads at that place',[24] which can only refer to the farmhouse. D'Erlon's own recollection on this point is also absolutely clear. 'The 2nd Corps,' he writes, 'must take the farm of Hougoumont and the 1st Corps must make itself master of La Haye Sainte, situated on the road to Brussels.'[25] The only light infantry regiment in the entire corps – the 13th – was given the task of capturing La Haye Sainte; its sapper companies were instructed then to fortify the buildings against an allied counter-attack.[26] Otherwise, no serious thought seems to have been given to the capture of the farmhouse. It may be that Napoleon expected the weight of d'Erlon's massed columns simply to submerge the buildings; it may be that he hoped that the capture of the ridge, and thus the flanking of the farm, would quickly render the garrison's position untenable. It may be that a preliminary shelling of the farmhouse was dismissed as a waste of resources given the limited calibre and number of guns available, and the difficulty of hitting a target partially concealed by a dip in the ground. His information on the farm was certainly imperfect, because it was only partially visible from his own position, and none of his informants, including General Haxo, had been able to get close due to the presence of enemy skirmishers. One way or the other, the failure to prepare the capture of La Haye Sainte more thoroughly was to cost him and his soldiers dear in the hours ahead.

4

Bolting the Barn Door

At around 11.30, Reille's 2nd Corps began its assault on Hougoumont. The defending Nassauers began to fall back, until reinforced by British Guardsmen. Over the course of the day, the contest was to suck in more and more troops on both sides. The men at the allied centre, as Captain Carl Jacobi of the Hanoverian Lüneburg Field (Light) Battalion recalls, were 'idle spectators for hours of the fighting that surged before [them] particularly of the violent contest around Hougoumont'.[1] At around 1 p.m., Napoleon's grand battery opened fire on the centre of the allied line. The bombardment had no particular focus: the guns did not target any specific area, but subjected the whole of it to a general softening up. Given the ranges involved, that was about all that was possible until the spur of ground in front of La Haye Sainte reconnoitred by the commander of the grand battery, Desales, had been secured against rifle fire from the farm. For now, the purpose of the cannonade was as much psychological as physical: the delivery of moral force to discourage the enemy from fighting.[2] Napoleon intended, as his order to Desales made clear, 'to astonish the enemy and shake his morale'.[3] It was 'shock and awe' tactics.

The emperor's plan met with mixed success. Bylandt's Netherlanders, who were deployed forward of the sunken road on the slope facing the French, suffered terribly. Most of the rest of the corps, however, were safe enough on the reverse slope, where they were protected from direct fire and where they lay down or crowded into ravines to reduce their exposure; they also benefited from the fact that the French cannon balls tended to stick in the thick mud rather than bounce to cause further destruction.[4] The light infantrymen, spread out in skirmish order along the allied front, lacked such cover but were sufficiently dispersed to avoid many casualties. One of the unlucky ones was Captain Philip Holtzermann of the 1st Light Battalion KGL, who was killed shortly after the bombardment began, at around the same time as his wife Mary-Ann was probably attending morning service in far-off Bexhill.[5] Over the course of the day his body was to be progressively ground into the soil beneath him.

Many of the projectiles fell in the vicinity of La Haye Sainte, which was only 700 metres or so from the forward French batteries.[6] The two allied artillery pieces on the road outside were quickly destroyed after engaging the French in a futile duel, against Wellington's strict orders. The men at the barricade scrambled for cover. Lieutenant George Simmons of the 95th Rifles had only just arrived with a pile of wood, in time to see the flight of 'young Germans [who] were so alarmed that they blunderingly crossed in front of the guns',[7] much to the amazement of more experienced men. In the sandpit nearby, Captain Johnny Kincaid of the 95th Rifles saw a French cannon ball, which 'came from the lord knows where', take 'the head off our right hand man'.[8] The British riflemen, most of whom had been under heavy artillery fire before, were neither shocked nor awed, however. Likewise, for the veteran garrison of the farm itself the cannonade was little more than an irritant. The men approaching the orchard were occasionally showered with branches shot off the tops of the trees by cannon balls passing overhead.[9] They were also at risk from splinters from explosive shells detonating above them. Otherwise, the sturdy masonry provided ample protection against the odd stray round. With the French assault imminent, Baring issued instructions to his company commanders: they were to hold on as long as possible, and then withdraw to the main allied line on the ridge behind.[10] The officers of the 2nd Light Battalion now went to their assigned posts – Lieutenant Meyer in the kitchen garden, Lieutenants Tobin and Graeme in the buildings, Baring himself to the orchard – and waited.

After about half an hour, the French guns fell silent. This was to enable the 1st Corps to begin the main attack on the allied centre. Adjutant-Major Hubart, an old soldier who had fought in all of Napoleon's campaigns, was charged with forming up the divisions. When all was ready, the corps commander, d'Erlon, placed himself at the centre of the line and called out 'We must vanquish or die today' ('*C'est aujourd'hui qu'il faut vaincre ou mourir*'). The men shouted back 'Long live the emperor ('*Vive l'empereur*'). Three drum beats now announced the order to advance. About 18,000 men moved forward, preceded by a cloud of musket-armed skirmishers. They advanced in columns one battalion wide and – accounts differ – nine or twelve battalions deep, a wider frontage than in the past. There is controversy about which formation was actually used.[11] D'Erlon, a veteran of the Peninsula, adopted this unusual formation over the more standard smaller-frontage columns in order to maximize French firepower against that of the feared British line formation he had encountered in Spain, while retaining some of the mass necessary to punch its way through with the bayonet. It left his corps more vulnerable to cavalry attack, however. The infantry advanced in divisional order with the left flank out in front, so that the attack would hit the allied line like a swinging door from left to right. Behind them came cavalry in support, including nearly 800 cuirassiers, heavy cavalry protected by the metal breastplates which gave them their name. Within a few minutes, the attackers had accomplished the complicated 'passage of lines', marching through their own artillery, without losing cohesion.[12] Behind them, the grand battery resumed its bombardment of the allied centre, its rounds now hurtling over the heads of the advancing columns. Those on the extreme left of the French advance – Aulard and Schmitz's brigades of General Donzelot's 2nd Infantry Division – were heading straight for the farmhouse of La Haye Sainte and would be the first to make contact with the enemy.

As they descended into the valley separating them from Wellington's line, the French columns came under heavy and continuous allied artillery fire; the German skirmishers, by contrast, began to withdraw. Corporal Canler remembers 'a terrifying duet conducted by the two batteries made up of close to two hundred guns: cannon balls, bombs, shells, passed and whistled above our heads'.[13] They had hardly advanced 100 paces when the commander of the 28th Ligne's 2nd Battalion, Marins, was mortally wounded. Canler's own company commander was struck by two rounds. Old Hubart and the eagle-bearer Crosse were also killed. It was more or less the same story across the French advance. We don't know for sure how the two brigades marching on La Haye Sainte fared, but the sapper companies in front – consisting of burly men with huge axes to batter down doors and barricades – must have suffered terribly not only from the allied shelling, but also from the rifles of the German skirmishers in the field to the left of the farm. Despite the punishing fire, however, all along the line the men heard the 'calm voice of our officers issuing the only command "close up"'.[14] Marshal Ney accompanied the column as far as the point where the road cut through the bank just before the farm.[15]

To the east of the farmhouse, the exposed Netherlanders of Bylandt's brigade began to fall back, but the riflemen in the sandpit stood their ground for the time being. Captain Leach, who had a ringside view, described the din and fury of the French advance 'as if the bare possibility of our being able to withstand the shock was out of the question'.[16] His battalion adjutant, Captain Kincaid, recalls a 'huge column of infantry' advancing with cheers of 'Vive l'empereur', 'carrying with them the *rubidub* of drums, and the *tantarra* of trumpets', their officers 'dancing and flourishing their swords in front'. The French, he wrote, 'had some hopes of scaring us off the ground', but were met only by a 'stern silence reigning on our side', waiting to show that 'we had mouths to open when we chose to use them'.[17] The Germans in the nearby farmhouse also showed no sign of anxiety. Napoleon's initial hope, to frighten them out of the buildings through artillery fire and the mere threat of massed infantry attack, had been disappointed.

In the orchard, they could hear the French – the thump of thousands of human feet and horses' hooves, as they churned up the muddy ground – but not see them. Then the first French skirmishers came over the slight elevation on the southern edge of the farm, cheering and loosing off a fusillade of bullets. Baring ordered the men to lie down, as they had so often before in the Peninsula, presenting a smaller target; the apple trees and low hedge of the orchard offered primarily psychological comfort. He himself, however, remained on horseback. Although hazardous, this was essential in order to give a good example to the men and maintain an overview of the battlefield. Baring gave strict instructions not to fire until the enemy was very close. Soon the two French main columns hove into view, moving fast. One attacked the buildings, while the other hurled itself into the orchard. 'The French are in such a hurry,' the Germans told each other, 'it is as if they wanted to eat in Brussels today.'[18] It was now that the riflemen opened a deadly fire from the skirmish line in the field beside the farm, the hedge behind the orchard, the barricade, the courtyard walls and the top windows of the house. We do not know exactly how many of Napoleon's men were killed at that moment, or throughout the day at La Haye Sainte; French sources estimate it to be as high as 2,000 all told by nightfall.[19] What we do know is that from this moment onwards, the ground around the farmhouse, and soon the buildings themselves, was strewn with bodies. The ubiquitous corpses were bad enough, but the sight and sound of the injured over the next five hours were even more distressing for those who witnessed them.

The French skirmishers in the orchard halted and took aim. A hail of bullets sliced through the reins of Baring's horse, missing his hand by inches, killed Rifleman Harz, thus vindicating his premonition, seriously injured one of the company commanders, Captain Schaumann, and killed and wounded many more. The musket-armed Frenchmen could keep up a much quicker rate of fire, probably two or three rounds a minute. The Germans could get off only about half that number, because their grooved rifle barrels were slower to load. Muskets, being smooth-bored, were unlikely to hit a man much more than ninety metres away, even if well aimed; rifles, with their grooved barrels, on the other hand, were accurate at nearly twice that distance. At close range, as in this initial clash, massed and repeated musket volleys were more effective, but for most of the rest of the day, when the riflemen were firing at the French at some distance from the cover of the farmhouse, the Germans had the advantage.

Both sides were now engaged in a process of attrition, in which they raced to aim, fire and reload.[20] This was done by holding the musket in the left hand (if right-handed), biting off the top of a prepared cartridge of powder and ball, retaining the ball in the mouth, and pulling the cock or hammer back a notch. Then the soldier pushed open the frizzen covering the firing pan, into which he poured some powder, before sealing it again. The musket butt was placed on the ground, allowing the rest of the powder to be poured vertically into the barrel, followed by the cartridge paper and the ball, either dropped or spat. The loader rammed the package down with his ramrod, once after the paper wadding, in order to compact and seal the package, and then after the ball. He then pulled the cock back another notch, took aim and fired. This released the flint, which struck the frizzen, producing a spark which set off the powder in the pan and in turn ignited the charge in the barrel, propelling the bullet. Rifles were loaded in a similar fashion. Sometimes, prepared paper cartridges were used, as with muskets. On other occasions, a pouch of lead balls and a powder flask were used. After pushing a measured charge of powder into the barrel, followed by a circular patch of greased cloth and the ball, the loader pushed down the package with his ramrod. The Baker rifle had a shorter barrel than the musket, making it easier to use from a prone position or in buildings, such as a farm.[21]

There were plenty of things that could go wrong, even in fine weather; all bets were off if it was wet. The hammer might be released accidentally before it was pulled back all the way, leading to a misfire known as 'going off at half-cock'. It was also possible that the flint would not produce a proper spark, or that the powder in the pan would simply not ignite, or that it would burn without setting off the charge in the barrel; the latter was known as a 'flash in the pan'. Sometimes, the weapons burst, injuring or even killing their owners. It was not uncommon to swallow the ball in the heat of battle, to spit it next to the barrel by mistake, to drop the cartridge, to spill the powder in it through clumsiness, to fire off the ramrod in error, or in the excitement to load and reload compulsively without actually firing. Even if the procedure passed off flawlessly, the infantryman was left with blackened lips and a gritty taste in his mouth that never quite went away and made him very thirsty.

Though the men in the orchard were completely outnumbered, they held their ground at first. The stricken Schaumann was dragged back to the relative security of the farm, where he soon after died of his wounds. Then the riflemen noticed that the French column on their right was quickly working its way towards the open barn door. Some of the skirmishers strung out in the field outside saw the approach of French cavalry and retired up the hill to the main position; others under Captain Hans von dem Busche took up position in a semi circle in front of the barn door to the west.[22] In the orchard, the Germans withdrew calmly, firing all the way. More men went down, including Baring's second-in-command, Major Bösewiel, who was mortally wounded, raising himself off the ground only to collapse once more. Young Ensign Robertson was killed with a bullet to the head, falling just beside Captain Biedermann. Baring himself made the safety of the barn, but his horse's leg was smashed by gunfire, and he was forced to take that of his adjutant. For now, the barn entrance was successfully held by von dem Busche's skirmishers, who shot down any approaching Frenchmen.

Meanwhile, the second French column – Aulard's brigade – approached the farm from the south-east, advancing 'obliquely ... over the fields as well as down the high road'. It quickly cleared the barricade on the road. Lieutenant Graeme and the other men holding it beat a hasty retreat into the courtyard via the main gate; Corporal Withelm Wiese recalls the bullets 'whistling around their heads'.[23] An intrepid and hirsute engineer – Lieutenant Vieux, a graduate of the Ecole Polytechnique – ran up and hacked furiously at the gate with an axe. When he was injured, and the tool slipped from his grasp, it was picked up by another man – but the gate stood firm. The rest of the blue tide crashed against the unyielding courtyard walls and stout wooden gate and swirled to the right up the road towards the main allied position. Bylandt's brigade, which had taken the brunt of the French cannonade, fell back in complete disorder; only one of five battalions held the line. The British riflemen in the sandpit and the

Germans on the eastern side of the house, however, had a perfect view of the advancing French, who were now raked from the front and left with accurate fire.[24] Sometimes, three or four attackers were felled by a single round, blasted at close range by powerful rifles through the loopholes in the wall, or from the piggery, on which about a dozen Legionnaires were posted. Using the angling of the dormer windows to deadly effect, marksmen picked off the French officers at will, often shooting beyond effective musket range. Unlike the Germans, who could at least bring their wounded indoors, the injured Frenchmen could only stagger back towards their own lines; many others lay writhing where they had fallen.

Despite this tableau of devastation, the French column ploughed on up the hill, driving the British riflemen out of the sandpit back to the main allied position. Some of the attackers now swung left and piled into the kitchen garden, held by Lieutenant Meyer's solitary company. The rest soon reached the ridge where they were hotly engaged by the British 5th Division, killing their famous commander, Thomas Picton, with a shot to the head close to the crossroads. The whole allied centre was now in immediate danger of being overrun.

Wellington, who had moved from Hougoumont with his staff to an elm tree near the crossroads at around 1.30 p.m., instantly realized the gravity of the situation. Either he, the Prince of Orange or General von Alten now

ordered the Hanoverian light infantry battalion of Lüneburgers to advance towards La Haye Sainte to support
Baring, while Colonel Ompteda's 5th and 8th KGL line
battalions were told to move up to the sunken road.[25] Wellington also instructed the 1st Light Battalion of the King's
German Legion to plug the gap to the left of the farmhouse. 'Now it is your time, my lads,' Captain Christoph
Heise, the acting adjutant of the battalion, heard him call
out to the Germans.[26]

Two companies of German light infantrymen, commanded by Captain von Gilsa and Lieutenant Albert,
surged out of the ravines where they had taken cover from
French artillery fire.[27] They raced over the road past abandoned British guns, formed up to the left and rear of the
French column and fired into the dense masses as fast as
they could reload. Others made for the kitchen garden.
Corporal Henry Müller positioned himself at the far end
in order to pick off the officer leading the French column.
Thanks to the help of riflemen Sasse and Schülermann,
who reloaded his weapons for him, he succeeded in knocking the Frenchman from his horse with a first shot.[28] The
enemy began to fall back. At this point Captain Heise was
badly injured in the leg, and was helped back towards the
allied line by a British rifleman, until the intense fire forced
him to abandon his charge. Luckily for Heise, Rifleman
Sander of the 1st Light Battalion now observed his captain's distress and dragged him to a steep bank, where

both men spent an anxious few minutes trying to avoid the attentions of prowling French cavalry.[29] Sander refused Heise's injunctions to save himself, and, when they were finally spotted by a French rider, the rifleman shot the horse from under him. Without taking off his weapon or backpack, Sander slung his superior over his shoulders and carried him to a surgeon at Mont-Saint-Jean before returning to the fray. Sander's dedication was remarkable, because it was well known that some uninjured Hanoverians, like many soldiers in all armies, were not above using the need to help a wounded comrade off the battlefield as an excuse to quit the fight altogether.[30]

As Ompteda's men pushed the French down the hill to the east of the farmhouse with fixed bayonets, he sent his adjutant forward though the smoke – which von Brandis recalls as being 'so thick that one couldn't see anything' – in order to establish whether they were facing enemy cavalry or infantry.[31] He almost immediately ran into a force of cuirassiers. The 1st Light and the 5th Line Battalions were covered by British cavalry nearby, and had time to form square, though Ompteda had a narrow escape when his horse was shot. Unfortunately, the 8th Battalion was still in line when the French struck and was routed in a few traumatic minutes, apparently without having had the opportunity, or at least the will, to resist. Its commander, Lieutenant-Colonel von Schröder, was mortally wounded. Captains von Voigt and von Westernhagen, Lieutenant von Marentholtz and more than thirty non-commissioned officers and men were rapidly killed. Many of the other officers were wounded, some badly. Ensign Moreau suffered three serious injuries and was forced to drop the colours close to the farm. Seeing this, Sergeant Georg Stöckmann of the 2nd Light Battalion ran out to retrieve the flag, and thus saved it from falling into enemy hands.[32] Major von Petersdorff managed to rally some of the men behind the sunken road, but the battalion was finished as a coherent fighting force and took no further part in the fighting.[33] It was the first of a number of object lessons that day in the danger which cavalry posed to infantry which had been caught in the open and unable to form square.

On the other side of the farmhouse all went well at first. The Lüneburgers advanced down the slope under the command of Lieutenant General von Klenke, though with more speed than good order.[34] They quickly pushed back the French. One company under Captain Jacobi recaptured the orchard,[35] and linked up with Baring's men who had re-emerged from the courtyard. The rest deployed in open formation in the fields outside to keep French skirmishers at arm's length. It did not take long, however, before another enemy column approached. Despite the efforts of twice-wounded Sergeant-Major Ludwig Schmidt to rally the men,[36] the low and skimpy hedges gave too little protection to enable a sustained resistance. The Germans in

the orchard fell back into the field outside, where they became caught up with the rest of the Lüneburgers. Suddenly,
a force of French heavy cavalry – cuirassiers commanded
by Colonel Crabbée – appeared out of a fold in the ground
and prepared to attack. At this very moment, Lieutenant
Meyer reported that the French had surrounded the kitchen
garden and made his position there untenable. Baring ordered him to retire to the house and to continue the fight
there, and then turned to face the enemy cavalry. In the din,
however, neither Baring nor von Klenke could make themselves heard in order to form square or at least some sort
of defensive perimeter. To make matters worse, the arrival
of the Lünebergers had disrupted the close formation of
von dem Busche's riflemen of the 1st Light Battalion KGL
outside the barn,[37] so that they too were unable to give effective covering fire.

It took only a few awful moments for the entire Lüneburg Battalion and the accompanying Legionnaires to be
completely dispersed. They do not seem to have put up
much of a fight. The cuirassiers were quickly on top of
them, hacking and slashing at the disordered infantrymen
with their swords. Some – such as the Lüneburgers Corporal W. Bühren, privates Fr. Pape, H. Schüler, J. Riese and
sC. Kloppe – made it to the safety of the farmhouse, where
they spent the rest of the day with the garrison. On the
way, Kloppe – who was already injured – managed to run
an enemy officer through with his bayonet.[38] Most headed

for the main allied line, exposing themselves not only to the swords of the pursuing cuirassiers, but also to the enfilading fire of the French infantry spilling out of the kitchen garden. Sergeant Schmidt suffered further injuries from cavalry swords. Von Klenke, too, was hurt. Some of the Germans were shot by their own side, hit by volleys which the squares fired at the approaching cavalry. Captain Biedermann describes how 'the men [in the main position] were already taking aim as I arrived at the square, so that I had no choice but to throw myself quickly to the ground and to crawl the last few paces [to safety]'.[39] Both von Klenke and Baring also made it, and together with the survivors took refuge in the brigade squares, where von Klenke's wounds were tended to – but many did not. Captain Jacobi had a miraculous escape, even though groups of enemy riders trotted past him only ten or twelve paces away. The trauma of the charge caused him severe temporary sensory deprivation. 'There were moments,' Jacobi recalled, 'when the senses of hearing and sight had in fact shut down, and not just figuratively so.'[40]

The French did not, however, capture the farmhouse and courtyard. As Baring looked on impotently from the main position, Lieutenants Graeme and Carey and Ensign Frank held out stubbornly with the rump of the battalion and some stragglers from the Lüneberg Field Battalion.[41] At this point, the defenders probably amounted to no more than a few dozen. The barn remained the site of furious contestation. Fortunately, the French did not try to climb up its walls, and the Legionnaires were able to snipe at them from the top of the pigsty. On the other hand, the men on the courtyard walls facing the road were frustrated by their own barricade outside, behind which the French were now taking cover. When Lieutenant Graeme nipped out of the side door which opened on to the road in order to observe the enemy, he was immediately set upon by three Frenchmen who disarmed him and tried to drag him away. Sergeant Diedrich Meyer came to his help, and succeeded in freeing Graeme, but received a musket blow to the head for his pains, was knocked out and himself taken prisoner.[42] Nearby, the French brought forward three twelve-pounder batteries flush with La Haye Sainte, to support d'Erlon's attack on the main allied line,[43] and perhaps also to batter the building into submission from close range. These moments were the nearest the farmhouse came to falling in the early afternoon.

Relief came from outside. The British Household and Union Cavalry Brigades charged the advancing and disorganized French. Within minutes, much of d'Erlon's corps – especially Aulard's brigade around La Haye Sainte – was fleeing down the slope back towards the grand battery. The three French twelve-pounders were quickly overrun, and it would be many hours before Napoleon succeeded in getting any guns that close to the buildings again. For a while the British riders were held up by French skirmishers

in the kitchen garden and sandpit, as well as French cuirassiers. The air resounded to the distinctive crash of
swords on helmets and breastplates: 'you might have fan-
cied it was so many tinkers at work', Lord Somerset recalled.[44] At around this time, the legendary boxer Corporal
Shaw of the 2nd Life Guards was unhorsed by a carbine
shot and crawled to the courtyard walls of La Haye Sainte,
where he bled to death. Soon, though, the enemy were
driven past the farm, where an exultant Lieutenant Waymouth of the 2nd Life Guards observed Lieutenant
Graeme still manning his post on the roof of the pigsty. As
they galloped further down the slope, the Household men
were blasted, but not deflected, by French skirmishers in
the orchard. Shortly after, the Life Guards and the cuirassiers became wedged between the two high banks of the
Genappe road just beyond the farm, before the British
cavalry hacked their way through.

Heartened by their success, and perhaps carried along
by natural momentum, the two brigades charged and temporarily overran the grand battery. Then – their formation
scattered and their horses 'blown' – the British horsemen
were in turn attacked by French lancers and very roughly
handled. Meanwhile, the French had scrambled into
square around the orchard of La Haye Sainte. The crisis
was over, but the net result of the action was to knock
most of d'Erlon's corps, and thus the majority of the
French infantry, out of the fighting until the late afternoon.

For the next few hours, much of the French centre was reduced to the role of spectators, while the officers tried to rally their men. Corporal Canler was one of those reduced for much of the rest of the afternoon to manning a picket line established to corral the fugitives and return them to their units. Only Durutte's division on the far right of the French line, furthest away from La Haye Sainte, was relatively unscathed.

The charge of the British cavalry greatly eased the pressure on La Haye Sainte, at least for a while. As the French infantry retired past the farm, Lieutenant Graeme led a sortie through the front gate. The Germans plunged their bayonets into the tightly packed enemy mass, 'like blind men in a rage', as Lindau recalled. The French were chased well beyond the barricade, where they soon surrendered when the cavalry caught up with them. Graeme guarded these men for a time, until the returning British hussars led them away to captivity.

Now that communication with the main position had been re-established, Baring returned to the farm, and the 95th Rifles sneaked back into the sandpit. The Legionnaires took up positions again behind the barricade, from where they traded fire with French skirmishers in the orchard and further down the slope. They now had an opportunity to survey the scene of carnage around the farm, which was 'literally covered' with dead and injured bodies, most of them from the enemy side. Lying dead or dying in the mud were Aulard himself, the brigade commander, Rignon, the commander of the 51st Ligne, Bonnet, the commander of the Second Battalion of the 105th Regiment and Marrens, the commander of the Second Battalion of the 28th Ligne, as well as many more junior officers and rank and file. At least as many were wounded. Lieutenant Graeme records that even his 'oldest soldiers' had 'never witnessed such a sight'.[45] He saw one poor Frenchman in a puddle who was so badly hurt that he ineffectually attempted to kill himself with his own sword, before being prevented by the riflemen; we do not know whether he survived.

The German wounded were carried to the casualty station in the recaptured kitchen garden, where they were tended to by surgeon Heise and his assistants. We have no records of their work, but it can only have been gruelling. A report by John Haddy James, the assistant surgeon of the 1st Life Guards, described 'the hasty surgery ... the awful sights ... the blood-soaked operating table ... the agony of an amputation, however swiftly performed, and the longer agony of a probing'.[46] Most of the wounds would have been from bayonets, sabres or musket rounds. The latter tended to punch rather than stab a victim, the soft-lead ball deforming on impact, shattering or tearing off limbs and frequently requiring painful amputations without any anaesthetic beyond alcohol. Very soon, the casualty station in the outhouse must have overflowed, and the less serious cases, and perhaps some of the hopeless ones as well, were probably propped up against the inside courtyard walls, where it was still relatively safe. We know that by the end of the siege wounded soldiers were also sent to lie on the beds on the first floor of the farmhouse itself.

Surveying the situation, Baring found his command much reduced. Three of his officers, Bösewiel, Schaumann and Robertson, were dead; six wounded; and some seventy of the rank and file were either killed, taken prisoner, still back behind the sunken road, seriously injured or otherwise incapacitated. At least one of his officers, Lieutenant Biedermann, did not return from the main position, and saw out the rest of the battle from one of the squares there.[47] At most 300 men of his original force remained, augmented by a few stragglers from the Lüneburgers, from von dem Busche's companies, and perhaps some of Spörcken's Hanoverian Jäger. Baring now requested reinforcements. Wellington reacted with the dispatch of two companies from the 1st Light Battalion, more riflemen, commanded by Captains von Gilsa and Heinrich von Marschalck. These were sent to the kitchen garden. Baring decided not to reoccupy the orchard, probably because he did not have enough men to hold such an extensive perimeter. He himself joined the rump of the battalion sheltering from the incessant shelling as best they could in the courtyard, and waited.

5

Inferno

By early afternoon Napoleon knew that he had a major problem on his hands. First he saw that the smoke was not moving forward around La Haye Sainte, but hung tenaciously like a cloud over the buildings. Then he observed the pell-mell flight of most of d' Erlon's corps. To make matters worse, Napoleon knew that there were Prussians approaching from the north-east. He therefore dispatched a strong cavalry screen to shield the right flank until Marshal Grouchy, who was now recalled from pursuing the Prussians, arrived. The emperor sent substantial infantry forces to keep the Prussians out of the village of Plancenoit on the eastern edge of the battlefield. His main headache, however, remained the stiff resistance put up by the

Germans in La Haye Sainte – Napoleon later estimated their numbers at an entire division, that is many thousands of men. The buildings formed a breakwater which shattered the cohesion of the French advance, and a bulwark which prevented him from bringing artillery up to blast the allied line at close range. Hippolyte Mauduit, who served as a grenadier in the Old Guard at Waterloo, recalls that it constituted a 'veritable outworks'.[1] The emperor needed more information. Perhaps for this reason, a daring lone cuirassier rode up to the barricade across the road which the riflemen had reassembled and reoccupied, peered over it and galloped off before the men manning it – who had assumed they were dealing with a deserter – had time to react effectively. Dodging the bullets they sent after him, the horseman must have reported that the position was still strongly held by the enemy.

The emperor's options were limited. Shelling the garrison into oblivion would take too long, at least with the calibre of guns – six- and twelve-pounders and 5.5-inch howitzers – available to him. The sturdy masonry of the farm could withstand most of what the grand battery could throw at it, at least for quite some time.[2] Its walls are so thick that even today a cordless landline phone cannot be used in it. His siege train of larger guns was too far away. Bringing up some light artillery pieces to break down the gate might theoretically have been possible, but would have been extremely risky in the face of unsuppressed rifle fire from the defenders; a similar deployment later in the battle led to the swift death of the gun crews at the hands of marksmen from the main allied line. There was nothing for it. The Germans would have to be dislodged by a direct infantry assault. There was a problem, however. Most of Reille's men were embroiled at Hougoumont, Napoleon could not commit Lobau's corps or the guard until he was sure of the Prussians, and much of d'Erlon's corps would remain a shambles for some time yet. Until they had been rallied, Napoleon could call only on Schmitz's men around the orchard, and bring across some of Durutte's forces from the right flank. Oddly, the as yet uncommitted division of Reille's 2nd corps on the the left, Bachelu's, remained, as its Chief of Staff Colonel Trefcon recalls, 'l'arme à bras [with ordered arms] in the same position. We were given no orders.'[3] Meanwhile, the French grand battery resumed its cannonade.

Wellington, for his part, now focused almost exclusively on his centre. He did not neglect Hougoumont, which was again reinforced, but he spent the rest of the battle close to the crossroads. Lambert's brigade was now moved up to behind the farm. The Prussians, too, could see the importance of the farmhouse. Count August von Thurn und Taxis, who was serving as the Bavarian liaison officer with Blücher, had a good view from the Prussian advance guard at Fichermont wood. The attack, he writes, 'was being made with great violence at La Haye Sainte in an attempt to force the English out by bursting through their centre. This would probably make a union of communication between our two armies impossible.'[4] For this reason, Thurn und Taxis recalls, Wellington began to send ever more urgent pleas to Blücher for help.

The respite in La Haye Sainte did not last long. Ney ordered another attack on the farm with 3,000 men. At around 3 p.m., two French columns appeared and assaulted both sides of the farm buildings at once. As before, the attackers raised a great din, yelling '*Vive l'empereur*', '*Avant mes enfants*' and other familiar cries.[5] This time, though, they advanced with some hesitation, perhaps unsurprisingly given their previous reception. Observing this, an infuriated Ney sent his ADC Octave Levavasseur forward with orders to tell them to get a move on. He found two companies of sappers taking cover behind a bank. Their captain – who clearly did not expect to survive the assault – handed Levavasseur his card, saying 'Monsieur aide de camp, take it, here is my name.' He then ordered the drummer to beat the charge, and the engineers surged forward to shouts of '*En avant*', followed by the waiting infantry.[6]

Baring recalls that he had never seen such desperate courage and ferocity in the enemy. The Germans behind the barricade kept the enemy skirmishers at bay for a while, but when the French main force appeared they risked being overwhelmed. Graeme once again led his men back to the farm, telling Private Lindau to close and bar the gate. Some of the riflemen now took it in turns to fire from the loopholes, stepping back quickly after each round to reload and enable another marksman to take aim. Others lined the stand on the courtyard walls and fired on to the road below and into the orchard. Once again, the massed French suffered terribly, but some of them managed to seize hold of the protruding rifles, or to shoot through the gaps in the wall themselves. A number of defenders at the loopholes and in the courtyard were felled this way; more tumbled from the courtyard firing steps above them. At one point, the French temporarily gained control of the loopholes. Five legionnaires drove them off: Corporal Riemstedt and Riflemen Lindhorst and Lindenau were injured in the charge, for which they were later decorated.[7] All the while, the enemy battered their axes furiously at the main gate, but they were unable to penetrate the stout oak.

Baring's weakest point was on the other side, where the missing door left the barn wide open to the field. Here the French piled in relentlessly, and were repeatedly shot down. Rifleman Ludwig Dahrendorf was one of those defending the barn; despite considerable loss of blood from three bayonet wounds, he refused to leave his post.[8] Riflemen Christoph Beneke, a straggler from the 1st Light Battalion, and Friedrich Hegener tried frantically to maintain the improvised barricade where the barn door had been; the latter suffered a bayonet wound to the leg in the process.[9] He too refused his officers' entreaties to retire from the fray in order to have his wounds seen to.[10] Baring counted seventeen dead enemy bodies, which soon provided a low wall behind which their comrades could shelter from the deadly German rifle fire.[11] Once again, Baring directed operations from horseback, despite the fact that he presented an inviting target in the cramped courtyard. Another horse was shot beneath him, and his orderly – convinced that his master was dead – rode off with the spare horses. Baring simply grabbed one of the many riderless beasts milling around. These struggles along the perimeter lasted about an hour. The Germans held firm, for now, but as the pressure mounted it seemed only a matter of time before the French burst through the gate, or the barn, or surged over the courtyard walls.

Once more, it was a cavalry attack which came to the aid of the garrison, this time a French one. At around 4 p.m. Marshal Ney, mistaking the redeployment of the allied main line to escape artillery bombardment as a sign of a general retreat, ordered successive cavalry charges on the allied line between Hougoumont and La Haye Sainte to attack the squares on the reverse slopes. Observers describe a 'boiling surf' of riders which swirled up the side and around the back of the farmhouse. As Captain William Siborne wrote, 'the whole space between La Haye Sainte and Hougoumont appeared one moving glittering mass'.[12] Behind La Haye Sainte, the men of the King's German Legion line battalions were in the thick of it, forming 'squares' of about 300 men each. Conditions in these formations – which could be a more or less perfect square of equal sides, or an oblong, or something altogether more ragged – were grim. The sergeants and officers shoved or cuffed the men, some of them mere frightened boys, back into formation each time musket or gunfire had opened the ranks, pausing only to check 'deception' or 'subterfuge' among those who had fallen to the ground.[13] The dead were thrown out in front, the injured cowered in the centre. In the middle of the square of the 5th Line Battalion, Surgeon Georg Gerson patiently tended to the wounded, including those of neighbouring Hanoverian formations, without regard to his own safety. His dedication and courage drew the admiration of the brigade commander, Colonel von Ompteda.[14]

Ney's thousands of cavalrymen never broke any of the allied squares, but the popular image of a futile tide of riders ineffectually lapping at the edge of a solid rock of infantry is misleading. Some of the French cavalrymen tormented the squares by firing pistols into them at close range, while skirmishers on horseback played on them with carbines, trying to tempt them into pointless volleys beyond effective range. The Germans responded by posting sharpshooters to drive them off.[15] In between attacks, Ney's riders took cover in the many folds in the ground, where they were often invisible from the main allied line. Meanwhile, their commanders took up positions on nearby hillocks in order to observe the enemy and to seize the moment when they could be caught on the move.

The result was a deadly game of rock, paper and scissors played out around the farmhouse throughout the afternoon and early evening. Ompteda's brigade had to disperse so as to escape the heavy artillery fire. 'In order to destroy our squares,' Lieutenant Wheatley of the 5th Line Battalion recalled, 'the enemy filled the air with shells, howitzers and bombs, so that every five or six minutes the whole battalion lay on its face, then sprang up again' when the danger had passed.[16] In order to confront d'Erlon's reformed infantry, however, it had to deploy in line. And in order to repel Ney's cavalry, they had to form square, which in turn rendered them very vulnerable to shelling. Here timing and judgement meant the difference between survival and disaster. Around 3 p.m., as the second French attack began, the 5th KGL Line Battalion was once again ordered forward to assist the defenders. Once again it was menaced by French cavalry, and it was only with some help from nearby British horsemen that the Germans were able to form square and avoid the fate of the 8th Line Battalion and von Klenke's Lüneburgers. On another occasion, they were rescued by KGL hussars.[17] In theory, this pattern could repeat itself indefinitely, but, whereas the Germans had to be lucky all the time, the French cavalry needed to be lucky only once.

As the cavalry storm raged around them, the farmhouse and its environs briefly became a little oasis of calm. Horsemen found it difficult to operate in the quadrilateral bounded by the barricade, sandpit, sunken road and the farm itself. The infantry assaults slackened a little during the charges, as the French foot soldiers made way for the horsemen to deploy. After the first failed assault, they withdrew disheartened along with the returning cavalry, the huzzas and jeers of the Germans ringing in their ears. For some vivid moments, Baring and his men had a ringside seat during the most dramatic events of the battle. He observed four lines of cavalry forming to the right in front of the farm: cuirassiers (heavy cavalry), followed by lancers (armed with long lances, as their name implies), then dragoons (technically mounted infantry but in practice heavy cavalry) and finally hussars (light cavalry).[18]

The defenders were not idle spectators, though. They knew that the riders were attacking their own divisional comrades on the reverse slopes, and that if they succeeded in that mission, another attack on the farm would not be long in coming. As the French cavalry passed the buildings, Baring ordered his men to concentrate all their fire on their exposed right flank. They raced out of the farm buildings to the west and poured fire into the enemy, presumably dodging back inside when any of them came too close. Numerous horses and riders were shot down, but 'without paying the least heed', the survivors pressed on towards the allied squares.[19] Sergeant Georg Stockmann distinguished himself by not only shooting a cuirassier officer's horse from under him, but also vaulting over the courtyard wall and taking the Frenchman prisoner under the fire and the eyes of the advancing enemy cavalry.[20]

It was not long, however, before the French renewed their infantry attacks. The German marksmen on the piggery and the courtyard walls blazed at them to terrible effect, particularly against their conspicuous officers. Private Lindau waged a personal vendetta against one commander, who had been directing the advancing columns. He had the Frenchman in his sights for some time, and eventually felled his horse, burying its rider under it. Not long after, the riflemen made another sally. The enemy nearest to hand were bayoneted; the rest fled. Lindau pursued them for some distance, until he saw the French officer, still pinned beneath his dead horse. The German grabbed his gold watch-chain and when the officer raised his sabre to stop him, Lindau brained him with a rifle-butt to the middle of his forehead. Swiftly, he cut loose the saddle bag, but when he turned to take his victim's gold ring events intervened. 'Get a move on,' his comrades called, 'the cavalry are making a fresh charge.' Lindau ran to the rest of the men, who drove off the enemy with a volley. Looking around the highway, he noticed to his satisfaction that the French dead were piled up 'more than a foot high' close to the barricade. In a gesture of mercy he paused to help a wounded man lying in a pool of water, crying out in pain with a bullet in his leg. Lindau grabbed his arms, while another rifleman took his legs, and together the two Germans carried the unfortunate to the courtyard wall, resting his head on the body of a dead comrade.[21] Lindau also managed to relieve an enemy of a purse stuffed with gold coins. When he offered his haul to Baring for safe-keeping, however, his commander refused. 'Who knows what lies before us today,' he replied. 'You must look after the money the best way yourself.'[22]

Shortly after, Lindau was shot in the back of the head. He refused Lieutenant Graeme's order to go back for medical attention. 'No,' he answered, 'so long as I can stand I stay at my post.' The rifleman soaked his scarf with rum and asked a comrade to pour rum into the wound and tie the scarf around his head. Lindau then attached his cap to his pack, reloaded his rifle and returned to the fray. Despite his injuries, he joshed with Lieutenant Graeme on the platform above, warning him not to expose himself too much. 'That doesn't matter,' the Scotsman responded, 'let the dogs fire.' Not long after, the lieutenant was wounded in the hand, which he bound up with a handkerchief. Lindau called out: 'Now Captain [sic] you can go back.' 'Nonsense,' Graeme replied, 'no going back, that won't do.'[23] That officer was a mere eighteen years of age.

In the kitchen garden, the reinforcements from the 1st Light Battalion saw off all French attacks. At the far end,

Corporal Diedrich Schlemm kept up a steady fire until a bullet in the lungs forced him to quit the fight. Corporal Henry Müller, one of the best marksmen in the battalion, continued his struggle against individual French officers, with the help of the two riflemen who reloaded his weapons between shots. This time he took aim at the commander of a column who approached waving his sabre and shouting '*avancez*'. When Müller killed the officer, his men immediately retired in disorder.[24] Yet another corporal, Friedrich Reinecke, was posted with ten men in a gap in the hedge from which he repelled repeated enemy attacks.[25]

Though heavily outnumbered, the riflemen had the advantage that the French line infantry found it difficult to bring their full volley fire to bear on a largely concealed and often prone enemy. They could often not even shoot unless the men in front of them were killed or stepped aside. Moreover, as light infantrymen, Baring's battalion were in their element at La Haye Sainte, often working in pairs as skirmishers had been trained to do. In relatively open ground, such as in the gardens, the man in front took aim and fired, while his partner reloaded, or covered him with a loaded weapon, before either moving forward, past his partner, or else waiting for his partner to fall back behind him, if the pressure up front was too great. This often created a bond between men, which became irrefragable over time, and contributed greatly to the cohesion and fighting power of light infantrymen.

Baring was deeply touched by the courage of his men. 'Nothing,' he recalled, 'could curb the valour of our people,' who 'laughed' in the face of danger. 'These are the moments,' he wrote, 'where one learns to sense what one soldier means to another and what the word comrade actually entails.'[26] When the fighting subsided a little around 5 p.m., however, it became clear that the garrison was in a parlous situation. Baring frantically set the men to work repairing the damage wrought by French artillery and infantry. More critical still was the fact that the intense fighting had consumed most of the ammunition with which the Germans had begun the struggle. Baring therefore dispatched an officer back to his brigade commander urgently requesting a fresh supply of rifle rounds. Ompteda had none to give him, however. The wagon with the battalion reserve had overturned during the retreat the day before, and the field depots had run short of rifle ammunition.[27] Besides, it was impracticable to move large quantities of cartridges into the farm as long as the main gate was exposed to direct French fire. Access via the back entrance was also problematic. 'Swarms' of enemy skirmishers, Edward Cotton recalls, had 'established themselves immediately under the crest of our position', where they 'cut off the communication between the farm and our main line'.[28] The British riflemen in the sandpit nearby had plenty of cartridges, and could literally have thrown them into the courtyard, but as they belonged to another brigade, Baring probably didn't ask them for any, and it is most unlikely that they were even aware of the shortage of bullets in the farmhouse.

By now, in any case, Baring faced a new problem. Shortly after Graeme was wounded, Lindau heard a cry from the barn: 'The enemy mean to get through here.' He took up position at the door, but Lindau had fired no more than a few shots when he suddenly noticed thick smoke under the beam. Despairing of penetrating, the attackers had set fire to the whole edifice. Luckily most of the straw had been removed for bedding the night before, but the blaze still spread rapidly. There was no shortage of water in the courtyard pond; the problem was that the Germans had nothing to carry it in. All the vessels and containers had been either burned overnight or ended up in one of the various barricades. Riflemen Wilhelm Wiese and Ludwig Dahrendorf immediately tore their caps off their heads, filled them with water and attempted to put out the fire, but to little avail. If the flames spread to the rest of the buildings, Baring would have to withdraw before his men were burned alive or asphyxiated by smoke.

By around 5 p.m., La Haye Sainte was the cause of intense concern. Napoleon was determined to take the farmhouse and blast his way through the allied centre before the Prussians arrived. It must have been around this time that he ordered Pegot's brigade across from Durutte's division on his right flank to launch another attack on the buildings. He also sent the Young Guard to throw the Prussians out of Plancenoit. Wellington, too, must have been concerned. Instead of a cascade of Prussians coming to his aid on the allied left wing, he now risked losing the battle in the centre while Blücher's men won it to the east. Conditions within the farm were growing critical. Quite apart from the burning barn, the constant shelling grated on the nerves of the garrison. The smoke, heat, dust and the constant biting of cartridges must also have made the men very thirsty. For the seriously wounded, the situation must have been little short of hellish, though slightly better than for the enemy casualties crawling or lying outside the farm.

Things were no better in the rest of the brigade. The 5th KGL Line were still formed in square close to the farm, beset alternately by artillery, infantry and cavalry, their situation growing ever more desperate.[30] Ammunition carts blew up nearby, maiming men and beasts. One eyewitness was 'shocked at the sight of broken armour, lifeless horses, shattered wheels, caps, helmets, swords, muskets, pistols' scattered about, 'still and silent'. Here and there, frightened riderless mounts would rush back and forth, trampling on the dead and dying; some of them stood on only three legs, their shattered limb dangling uselessly. Several of these were shot to put them out of their misery, and Lieutenant Wheatley observed that 'it would have been an equal charity to have performed the same operation on the wriggling, feverish, mortally lacerated soldiers as they rolled on the ground'.[31] 'Because of the nature of the terrain', and because it was exposed to diverse threats, the battalion journal records, the 5th Line Battalion 'was forced to remain mobile, sometimes forming square and sometimes deploying [in line]'.[32] French cavalry charged no fewer than five times, on occasion retiring out of range into a fold in the ground in front of the Germans. Their commander would then take up position on a nearby elevation and order his men forward again whenever he spotted an opportunity to catch the enemy unawares. Ompteda, who had taken refuge with the 5th Line Battalion after his horse was killed, asked several of his men to shoot down the French commander, but none was able to do so. After the fifth charge, he finally turned to Rifleman Johan Milius, a straggler from the 1st Light Battalion, who lay injured in the square, having been hit in the leg by grapeshot. He volunteered to have a crack, and after being carried to a firing position by several comrades, Milius blasted the unfortunate French colonel off his horse with his second shot.[33]

Shortly after 5 p.m., the French launched another massive two-column attack on the farmhouse, now shrouded in smoke from the burning barn.[34] At around this time, one of Wellington's adjutants rode up to order what was left of Ompteda's brigade forward to engage the French columns moving on La Haye Sainte. The commander of the 5th Line Battalion, Lieutenant-Colonel von Linsingen, immediately gave an instruction to his men to deploy forward in line. Hardly had he done so, however, than French cavalry reappeared and menaced his right flank. Fortunately, they were set upon by nearby British Life Guards. Just in time, the 5th Line Battalion formed square and the danger passed. Presently, another adjutant appeared from the direction of La Haye Sainte. 'Fifth Battalion deploy and advance,' he called urgently from far off in order to relieve pressure on the farm. Ompteda stepped out of the square and asked him amiably whether 'it might not be best to advance in square and form line only when they were close to the enemy infantry'. Given their recent close shave with French cavalry this was sensible advice, but it would have slowed down the battalion considerably. 'God damn it,' the adjutant shot back brusquely, 'my order is to order you to deploy immediately', presumably because the situation in La Haye Sainte would admit of no delay. Piqued by his interlocutor's tone, Ompteda turned on his heels in formal military manner and gave the order to deploy. Once again, the French cavalry appeared out of the blue, and this time the friendly horse regiment detailed to cover the 5th Line Battalion was nowhere to be seen. It was only with great difficulty that the battalion was able to form square in time and repel the enemy, who had advanced to within eight paces of them.[35] For the third time, the luck of the 5th Line Battalion had held.

Ompteda now had a chance to consider Baring's request for help. In the absence of ammunition, he sent to the farm the next best thing: the light company of the 5th Line Battalion under Captain von Wurmb. The weakened battalion watched them leave with trepidation.[36] The rump had now shrunk to a mere 227 men.[37]

En route, Wurmb's company was raked by French artillery as they crossed the field which separated them from the farm. Wurmb himself was hit by a cannon ball and killed outright, another fourteen or so men were also slain, and Ensign Walther suffered a light injury. The rest, about eighty-five effectives, made it to the buildings.[38] As line soldiers, their standard issue British red uniforms marked them out from Baring's green-jacketed men. They were also equipped with muskets, whose ammunition was not compatible with rifles. Baring therefore dispatched another officer with a still more urgent request for more ammunition. Instead Ompteda sent 200 Nassauers from the 'Flanquer-Compagnie' of the 1st Regiment.[39] The commander, Captain von Weitershausen, was killed on the way to the farm.[40] The rest seem to have arrived safely, but because they were equipped with muskets, they brought no additional rifle rounds. Baring posted both groups of men in the courtyard.[41]

The Nassauers soon proved their worth. Baring immediately noticed that they carried large field kettles, and realized that these could be used to put out the fire in the barn. He tore one off the back of a passing soldier, filled it with water and threw it on to the barn. He was joined by Sergeant Reese from Tündern and Rifleman Poppe. Many officers, especially Lieutenant Carey, followed their example and soon the entire courtyard garrison joined in, so that within a few minutes all the field kettles were in use. Even the wounded rank and file threw themselves into the task. 'So long as our officers fight and we can stand,' they announced, 'we will stand our ground.'[42] It was hazardous work because the loopholes in the courtyard walls behind them were weakly held, and the French were able to fire at the Germans as they refilled their kettles with water. At the cost of more casualties, including Reese, who was felled by the pond mortally wounded, the fire was extinguished, at least for the moment.

Lindau and some of his comrades, noticing that the French musketry had slackened, now tried to retake the loopholes. Just as he had discharged his weapon, however, it was grabbed by one of the attackers. 'Look,' Lindau remarked to his neighbour, 'the dog has seized my rifle.' 'Wait,' the comrade responded, 'I have a bullet,' and shot down the Frenchman. When another assailant tried his luck, he was stabbed in the face by Lindau's neighbour on his right. Drawing his rifle back to reload, Lindau felt a fusillade of bullets whistle past him, hitting the stone wall;

one blew the wooden tuft from his shoulder, another shattered the cock on his rifle, so that it could no longer be fired. Casting around for a new weapon, Lindau ran to the pond where Reese lay dying, but when he tried to take his rifle – which was known to be very accurate – Reese pulled such a face that Lindau relented and found another nearby. He returned to the loophole at the courtyard walls but soon ran out of bullets again.[43]

Corporal Riemstedt and Riflemen Lindhorst and Lindenau also continued to stand their ground in the courtyard, despite their injuries. Once they ran out of bullets, they used their sword bayonets (*Hirschfaenger*), clubs (*Knittel*) and even stones as weapons. When the enemy tried to take aim at the men in the courtyard through holes in the masonry, the three pressed themselves against the wall to get out of the line of fire, and smashed the protruding guns out of their attackers' hands. When Baring suggested that Lindau should retire to have his injuries seen to, Lindau responded that he would not leave his commander's side 'so long as his head was on his shoulders'. Likewise, Sergeant Friedrich Wittop insisted on holding his position despite injuries to a hand and arm, as did Rifleman Philip Sandvoss, who was badly injured in the chest, and Corporal Ludwig Fabian, who also held his ground despite serious wounds. As they ran out of bullets, the Germans rifled the pockets of their dead and wounded comrades for more rounds, while Baring rode around on his horse reassuring the men that fresh supplies were on their way.

Some time between 6 and 6.30 p.m., the French withdrew once more; their latest attack had lasted nearly ninety minutes. The exhausted Baring found that his men were down to an average of three or four rounds a piece. He now sent another officer with a third request for more ammunition, warning that he would otherwise be forced to abandon the farm. Morale remained high. In the lull in the fighting, the men rushed to repair damage from artillery fire and defiantly proclaimed their determination to fight on. 'No man will desert you,' they cried out to their commander, 'we will fight and die with you.' At the same time, however, they pointed out 'sarcastically' that they could not hold on for much longer without bullets to fire back at the French.[50] 'No pen, not even that of a man who has experienced such a moment, can describe the feelings which now welled up in me,' Baring recalled. 'I had never felt so exalted,' he wrote later, 'but I had also never been in such a cruel situation where honour competed with concern for the survival of soldiers who were showing such confidence in me.'[51] These declamations were thus also a plea, part of a three-sided negotiation now taking place between Baring, his men and his brigade commander outside. Baring had to weigh the defence of a vital post, the

expectations of his superiors and the conventions of courage against the lives of the men for whom he bore sole responsibility. The shortage of ammunition offered a golden
bridge over which he and his Germans could retreat, their
honour intact.

6

Hand to Hand

The struggle for La Haye Sainte, and thus the battle as a whole, was reaching its climax. At around six in the evening, the Germans outside the farm passed the word down the line that the Prussians were coming. Their spirits surged. Looking to his left, Lieutenant Wheatley saw 'a dark swarm moving out of a thick wood'.[1] Whether they would arrive in time and in sufficient force to make a difference in the allied centre was not clear, however. By now, most of d'Erlon's men had been rallied for a renewed attack there. It would be spearheaded by an assault on the farm led by the 13th Light Infantry Regiment, some sappers and Pegot's infantry brigade. Wellington, now deeply worried about the shortage of ammunition in La Haye

Sainte, rode closer to the farm to see for himself. Meanwhile, the position of the Germans in the buildings was desperate. Their commander knew that they did not have enough men or bullets to hold off another determined attack.

Baring had little time to reflect on his predicament, because the French once again attacked in two mighty columns. For the fourth and last time, Baring sent an officer back to Ompteda with a frantic request for more ammunition,[2] and warning in the most drastic terms that he would have to quit the farm without it, but none came. He then turned to face the attackers. The French initially concentrated on the barn, where they reignited the fire.[3] The Germans succeeded in putting it out again. As their fire slackened due to a lack of bullets, the French were emboldened to climb on the walls and on to the roof of the barn and stables. From there they could shoot down the defenders in the courtyard with impunity, as the Germans were able to return fire only very intermittently. Others streamed over the walls and jumped into the courtyard. Lindau ran one attacker through with his bayonet, who promptly collapsed on top of him, twisting the blade so badly out of shape that Lindau had to throw it away.[4] Presently, the French surged through the open barn door, which could no longer be held; its defenders, including the intrepid Lindau, fell back into the courtyard.

To make matters worse, the Germans were also assailed by a second wave of attackers who hurled themselves against the main gate. The French ripped away the rifles which the defenders had aimed through the loopholes. Despite this, dozens of attackers were shot down as they approached the courtyard walls. A breach was eventually made in the main gate.[5] As they entered, however, the leading attackers were individually bayoneted, and the rest at first thought better of following. The cry went up among the garrison: 'Defend yourselves, defend yourselves! They are coming over everywhere. Come together.'[6] A short stand-off now developed in the courtyard, as the French and Germans faced each other over the cobblestones.

Baring knew that the position of the garrison had become untenable. With the enemy pouring into the courtyard through the barn and the main gate, and with his men down to their last rounds of ammunition, further resistance was pointless, and retreat was no disgrace. Baring gave the order to withdraw. 'Only he who has been in the same situation,' the commander recalled, 'can judge how much these words cost me and with what feelings they were accompanied.'[7] The retreat would take careful timing, however, and depended on holding the kitchen garden on the other side of the house. Baring was worried that a precipitate scramble would unsettle the defenders there and cause them to abandon a position which might still be held. For this reason he left Lieutenants Graeme and

Carey, as well as Ensign Frank the 'honour' – and thus the potential death sentence – of covering his retreat and being the last men out. Baring exited through the narrow passageway and quickly conferred with his officers in the kitchen garden. Finding the situation there too precarious, he told the men to make individually for the main allied position. The company in the garden, or what was left of it, withdrew under the command of Corporal Müller, Lieutenant Meyer having been wounded and all other officers presumably either dead, injured or absent.[8] The French let them go.

Lieutenants Carey and Graeme, Ensign Frank, Sergeant-Major Mevius, Sergeant Wilhelm Stegen, Corporal Heinrich Heise, Riflemen Lindhorst and Lindenau and private Friedrich Breithaupt now drew themselves up to hold the house and give their commander and the rest of the garrison time to escape.[9] Given the shortage of ammunition, this was no easy task, and within no time the French were firing down the passageway. When one of them tried to shoot Frank, Lieutenant Graeme ran him through the body with a sword, and sliced a second unfortunate in the face. The favour was soon returned. As one of the attackers levelled his weapon at Lieutenant Graeme, Ensign Frank called 'take care', but the Scotsman simply replied 'never mind, let the blackguard fire'.[10] Luckily for him, the Frenchman was still taking aim when Frank stabbed him in the mouth and through the neck with his sabre, so that he fell to the ground at once. Almost immediately, another assailant shattered Frank's arm with a bullet just above the hand, rendering him defenceless. Graeme was now cornered by four men and an officer, who seized him by the collar exclaiming, 'That's the rogue' ('*C'est ce coquin*'). The men thereupon levelled their bayonets and 'made a dead stick at Graeme, who parried the thrusts with his sword. He noticed, however, that the French, no doubt drained after a traumatic afternoon, 'all looked so frightened and pale as ashes'. Graeme tore himself free, bolted through the lobby followed by a fusillade of shots and curses, and ran to safety.

The rest of the rearguard were not so fortunate. Corporal Heise, who was a straggler from the 5th Line Battalion, was struck on the head during the mêlée and taken prisoner.[11] So were one corporal and seven enlisted men of the Nassauers.[12] There was now no holding the French, who piled into the farmhouse. Frank was hit by another bullet in the chest and staggered into a room, where he hid behind the bed.[13] His pursuers did not see him, but no quarter was given to two wounded soldiers who were lying there. 'Take that for the fine defence you have made,' the French cried before shooting them. In the courtyard, Lindau was suddenly surrounded by the French. Taking his weapon by the barrel he swung the butt against them. The sound of curses filled the air: '*Couyons Hanovriens*' and '*Anglais*'. A Frenchman seized him by the front, and the two men wrestled. When another attacker thrust him with his bayonet, Lindau parried it by swinging his first assailant around. Inadvertently stabbed by his own side, the Frenchman fell to the ground crying 'my God, my God'.[14] The German raced to the barn hoping to get out that way, but found his path blocked by the enemy. He then jumped over a fence, and was immediately made prisoner along with Captain Adolf Holtzermann, brother of the unfortunate Philip, who had been killed shortly after the battle commenced, and a number of others. For Rifleman Lindau, at least, the battle was over.

There was no rest for the men who made it out of the farmhouse. Lieutenant Carey was injured in the retreat, further reducing the number of officers. Rifleman Dahrendorf, who had already suffered three bayonet wounds and was losing blood steadily, now took a grapeshot round in his left leg.[15] Surgeon Heise made it out safely, and set up a new casualty station further back. Baring sent what was left of the reinforcements and stragglers back to their own formations, and rallied the remnant of his battalion. This was no easy task, because several officers had been killed in the farmhouse, others had been captured and some of the rest were injured. Baring now joined two companies of the 1st Light Battalion in the sunken road under the command of Lieutenant Colonel Louis von dem Busche, providing them with critical mass, even though they had nothing with which to fire at the French.[16] No sooner had Graeme caught up with him at the main position than they were charged by cuirassiers. The lieutenant and his men scrambled into a hollow, from which they 'peppered' the French cavalry, their rifle bullets penetrating the thick breastplates, probably having been resupplied with ammunition by their comrades in the 1st Light Battalion.[17]

The tactical value of the farmhouse now became clear. 'The loss of La Haye Sainte,' Captain Johnny Kincaid of the 95th Rifles in the nearby sandpit recalled, 'was of the most serious consequence, as it afforded the enemy an establishment within our position.'[18] 'The house was instantly filled with the enemy's infantry,' Captain Jonathan Leach remembered, 'for several hours afterwards they kept up a dreadful fire from loopholes and windows in the upper part of it, whereby they raked the hillock so as to render it untenable by our [British rifle] battalion'.[19] Enemy skirmishers also put up a firing step along the wall and – as one eyewitness recalled, 'cut holes in the garden hedge, resembling windows'.[20]

Ney demanded fresh troops to exploit the breakthrough. Napoleon famously replied: 'Troops, where does he expect to find troops? Does he expect me to make them?' All the same, substantial French infantry formations now moved up towards the farm and a battery of horse artillery was brought to an elevation near the buildings from where they could blast the allied position at close range (300 metres), the first time since they had unsuccessfully attempted to do so in the early afternoon.[21] 'A knowing, enterprising fellow holding the post of La Haye Sainte, which we had lost,' one British officer from Peck's brigade later wrote, 'sent a strong detachment, which got to the hillock under cover of the brow, and opened a kind of masked battery on us.'[22]

The French cavalry, taking advantage of hollows and folds in the ground near to the farm, swarmed with fresh vigour.[23] The British riflemen in the sandpit were driven off once again, allowing the enemy to shoot at the men in the sunken road from a distance of only eighty metres. Large numbers of allied officers were struck down in quick succession. One British infantry regiment at the crossroads, the Ulstermen of the 27th Inniskillings lost more than two-thirds of all its men in the battle, the highest proportion of any comparable formation at Waterloo. It was, as Johnny Kincaid remembers, 'lying literally dead in square'. 'I had never yet heard of a battle in which everybody was killed,' he adds, 'but this seemed likely to be an exception as all were going by turns.'[24]

Captain Shaw-Kennedy, who was serving on the quartermaster-general's staff, recalled that after the loss of the farm 'the danger was [now] imminent; and at no other time of the action was the result so precarious as at this moment'. Because the Hanoverians and Legionnaires in Kielmannsegg and Ompteda's brigades had suffered so badly, a dangerous gap was opening up in the centre between

Halkett and Kempt's brigades. Shaw-Kennedy galloped to Wellington to warn him that the French troops pouring up the road past La Haye Sainte were well placed to punch through his weakened centre.[25] The whole battle hung in the balance.

It was not long before the French pressure began to tell on the Germans in the sunken road. Captain von Marschalck, who had brought one of the reinforcing companies to the farmhouse, was killed, and Captain von Gilsa's right shoulder was shattered.[26] Lieutenant Albert was also killed. Graeme tried to rally the men by swinging his shako in the air and calling to them, but his hand was smashed by a bullet. Baring himself continued to provide encouragement by riding around on a dragoon horse whose saddle was festooned with large pistol holsters and covered by a blanket. The fire was so intense that four bullets struck the blanket and another blew his hat off his head. When Baring dismounted to retrieve it, a round slammed into the saddle he had just vacated; his luck held once again.

Nearby, the 5th Line Battalion of the King's German Legion still stood its ground. It was exposed to heavier enemy fire after the fall of La Haye Sainte, killing the adjutant, Lieutenant Schuck. The square was now so shrunken that there was not enough space for the entire brigade staff, so Ompteda stepped outside and handed command of the battalion back to Lieutenant-Colonel

Linsingen.[27] When Ompteda's horse was felled by a cannon ball in the chest, Ompteda asked his *aide de camp* to lend him his mount. Brandis then set off to the rear in order to find a replacement. There he found everything in confusion, with the reserve mounts nowhere to be seen, but he managed to bag a captured French cuirassier horse from a surgeon of the 2nd Light Battalion. Hardly had Brandis mounted the beast, however, than a cannon ball took off one of its front legs. He fell next to a dead British cavalryman and the corpse of Captain Philip Holtzermann, killed at the start of the siege of La Haye Sainte, whose body was ground into the mud and almost unrecognizable. Brandis had to double back and find one of the reserve horses, which took some time, before riding back post-haste to the brigade. He made slow progress along the road, however, as it was clogged with shot-up artillery and other carriages as well as injured and unwounded cavalry and infantry, all seeking to escape the incessant shelling.[28]

Meanwhile, Rifleman Lindau's captivity was proving no less hazardous. The French were in a foul mood on account of the casualties they had suffered taking La Haye Sainte. When one German prisoner would not move quickly enough on account of his wounds, he was bayoneted in the groin. His outraged comrades crowded around. It took all of Captain Ernest Augustus Holtzermann's energy to pacify the situation, which might easily have ended in a massacre. The Germans were now herded out of the barn, across the courtyard, through the main gate and down the highway towards the French lines. They were mobbed by enemy soldiers, who grabbed Lindau's bag of gold coins and his three watches (one gold and two silver), falling out among themselves over the spoils. When his last possession had been taken, Lindau became so enraged that he punched in the face a Frenchman who continued to search him. At that moment, the group was struck by two allied cannon rounds which swept away Frenchman and German alike.[29]

The situation in the allied centre was now critical. Accurate rifle fire soon silenced the nearby French gunners, but a more concerted effort would be needed to hold back the infantry and drive off the skirmishers. The corps commander, the Prince of Orange, and the divisional commander, General von Alten, now decided to send forward the 5th Line Battalion to repel the French and perhaps recapture the farmhouse. This made military sense in theory, and indeed Sir James Kempt, who had taken over command of the neighbouring division when Picton was killed, seriously considered dispatching the 27th Infantry Regiment to recapture the tactically vital farm.[30] In practice, however, the under-strength KGL battalion was far too weak for the job, and with the whole area infested with French cavalry the task was nothing short of suicidal. It was for this reason that Kempt decided not to order any of his men to break square and attack the buildings, but neither Alten nor the Prince of Orange seems to have had any such reservations. When the prince's adjutant, Lord Somerset, arrived to order the advance, Ompteda pointed out that the British cavalry, which had been posted behind them, had now been sent to the right flank and that the French cuirassiers, whose helmets they could clearly see in the hollow in front of them, would therefore attack the battalion as soon as it deployed in line. It was a tense conversation, the third or fourth such exchange which Ompteda had had that afternoon. Somerset galloped back to the corps staff.

Presently, the prince himself appeared, along with Alten. The divisional commander, an experienced soldier and an old friend of Ompteda, repeated the order. Ompteda in turn reiterated his concerns, adding that he should at least be supported by cavalry to deter enemy cuirrassiers. The Prince of Orange then interjected that the riders in the hollow were Dutch. Even though he was eventually convinced to the contrary, the prince was not to be moved. 'I must repeat my order,' he announced peremptorily, 'for an attack in line with the bayonet. I forbid any further objections.' To Ompteda, who was an emotionally unstable man at the best of times, the implied suggestion of cowardice – for the second or third time that day – was unbearable. He shouted out loudly: 'Well I will', drew his sword and told the battalion to form line. Knowing that they were marching to near-certain death, Ompteda turned to the battalion commander, Lieutenant-Colonel von Linsingen, and said, 'Try to save my two nephews.' He meant the sixteen-year-old Christian Ludwig von Ompteda and Ludwig Albrecht von Ompteda, who was only fourteen, both temporarily assigned to the 5th Line Battalion. Then he rode to the head of his men and led them against the enemy.

In a trice, the battalion had cleared the sunken road and beheld a medley of enemy infantry, cavalry and artillery between the ravine and the northern edge of the kitchen garden. Braving the murderous musket fire, Ompteda called out to his men: 'Follow me, brave comrades', and with a 'hurrah' they stormed forwards as quickly as they could over ground which was still muddy from the rain and had been churned up by successive waves of infantry and ploughed by numerous artillery barrages.[31] Inspired by the sound of the bugle and the 'thrill' of the moment, Lieutenant Wheatley swept past Ompteda. 'That's right, Wheatley,'[32] the commander cried. Within moments, however, they were assailed from the right and rear by cuirassiers hiding in one of the hollows. In a few terrible minutes the battalion was virtually destroyed. Wheatley was knocked unconscious. Linsingen was buried under his injured horse. When he finally extricated himself, he saw Ompteda's two nephews, Christian and Ludwig nearby.

Linsingen grabbed the two teenagers by the epaulettes and, much against their will, whisked them back to the sunken road. Twelve officers, twelve sergeants, a drummer and 128 men lay dead or seriously injured; the rest were dispersed in all directions. The luck of the 5th Line Battalion had finally run out.[33]

Ompteda himself rode unhesitatingly to a lonely death. Witnesses report seeing his distinctive white plume approach the French lines on horseback, and the enemy infantry taking aim at the solitary figure. Their officers, moved by the nobility of the gesture, pushed up the barrels of the men's muskets with their swords. Soon Ompteda reached the French line at the north edge of the kitchen garden and leapt into it. Captain Berger, one of the surviving company commanders, saw him strike off a number of French shakos with his sword. Still the French officers looked on without intervening. Then Berger glanced behind him to where his battalion had been and found himself completely alone on the battlefield. When he turned back towards the French, he caught a glimpse of Ompteda, who had eventually been shot at close range through the neck, falling from his horse and disappearing into a throng of enemy infantry and cavalry.[34] The three-sided clover leaf which had held the three Ompteda boys together through thick and thin had finally been torn apart.

When he came to, Wheatley found himself bare-headed in a ditch with a 'violent headache'. Ompteda lay dead nearby, with a hole in his throat. Wheatley tried to escape the Frenchmen rifling through the pockets of the casualties, but when he got up he was so disoriented that he immediately collapsed and was seized by an enemy with the words 'Where are you going, dog?' Wheatley was dragged to La Haye Sainte, where he found a scene of utter devastation. The insides of the buildings were 'completely destroyed, nothing but the rafters and props remaining'. The floor was strewn with the corpses of Baring's men and their French assailants. A major in green, probably Bösewiel, lay dead close to the door. A small part of the main gate was found to have no fewer than eighty musket balls embedded in it. 'The carnage had been very great in this place,' Wheatley records.[35] 'The entire edifice,' another eyewitness writes, 'was a scene of ravage and desolation.'[36] Unknown to either prisoners or captors, the wounded Ensign Frank was still hiding under the bed upstairs in the farmhouse.

The survivors of the 5th Line Battalion joined the remnants of the 1st and 2nd Light battalions in the sunken road, where Brandis finally caught up with them, distraught at news of the death of his commander. Nearby, the rest of the shattered brigade, the rump of the 8th Line Battalion, stood in square. Emboldened by their success over Ompteda's men, the cuirassiers charged at the main allied force. Baring's riflemen blasted them at twenty metres from concealed positions in the sunken road, and the cavalrymen were driven off to the jeers of the Germans. At this moment, the 3rd King's German Legion Hussar Regiment appeared, which prompted the cuirassiers to reform with astonishing rapidity to confront them. There was a brief stand-off as the two groups of riders eyed each other warily, until the hussars surged forward and Baring's jaded riflemen were faced with a mêlée just 200 paces in front of them. It was brief, but very bloody. Then both sides withdrew, the hussars passing through Baring's lines.

He and his men were then witness to an extraordinary interlude. A hussar corporal had been surrounded by cuirassiers and swept back with them, before breaking free and making his way towards his comrades. A cuirassier had met the same fate among the hussars, with the result that they met roughly halfway between the two lines. Even though the hussar was already bleeding heavily, the two men went for each other hammer and tongs under the eyes of both sides. Nobody moved to interrupt the fight. Baring feared for the injured hussar, but his skill won out over the brute force of the Frenchman, who was run through the face with one blow, and then knocked completely off his horse with the second. The hussar then returned calmly to his regiment, to the applause of Baring's men.[37]

Napoleon now staked everything on a last throw. The Prussians were arriving in large numbers on his right flank and could no longer be stopped. If he could plough through the allied centre and crush Wellington at the crossroads, however, the emperor could still save the day. The Imperial Guard were sent up the road towards La Haye Sainte, before wheeling left, attacking the allied line between the farmhouse and the château of Hougoumont. On their right flank, d'Erlon's 1st Corps, or what had been reassembled after the British cavalry charges in the early afternoon, climbed the slope on the east side of La Haye Sainte to attack the crossroads. They advanced slowly, in column square to be ready for all eventualities.

The first of d'Erlon's columns, led by the fresh men of Pegot's brigade, soon hit what was left of Ompteda's forces around the sunken road. By now, the whole area behind the farm 'was strewn with wounded', as one British cavalry officer recalls, 'over whom it was barely possible to avoid moving. Wounded or mutilated horses wandered or turned in circles. The noise was deafening, and the air of ruin and desolation that prevailed wherever the eye could reach gave no inspiration of victory.'[38] Brigade Adjutant von Einem was hit in the abdomen by a musket ball. As he fell on to the neck of his horse, he called out: 'I am done for.' He then asked Brandis to take his watch and money for safe-keeping. Brandis refused, encouraged him to hang on and brought the stricken adjutant on horseback to a nearby Hanoverian square, where four men carried him away in a blanket.[39] The divisional commander General von Alten was injured. At around the same time, Baring lost his third horse, which took a bullet to the head and fell on top of him, pinning his right leg to the ground in the deep clay. It took some time for a rifleman to emerge from the sunken road to help him. Baring managed to get out from under the horse, but his leg – though not broken – was out of action. He begged his men to fetch him another horse, offering them large sums of money to do so.

After more than five hours of almost constant fighting, and about half an hour after they had abandoned the farm, Baring's command began to crumble. Unwounded soldiers headed for the rear area 'in search of ammunition'. The officers and men ignored Baring's pleas for a horse. 'People who called themselves my friend,' he recalled bitterly, 'forgot this word and thought only of themselves.'[40] Brandis ran into Baring as he stood 'completely isolated without a single man of his battalion'.[41] Eventually the commander of the 2nd Light Battalion staggered to a house behind the line, where an Englishman caught one of the riderless horses crashing around, provided it with a saddle and helped him to mount up. He then rode back to the sunken road, but found that his men had left, supposedly to find more bullets. Right and left of Baring, men from two newly formed Hanoverian infantry battalions were running away in panic, accompanied by their remaining officers. After a vain attempt to appeal to their honour, he struck down one of them with his sword to restore order. But his comrades merely streamed to left and right of him, shouting to the men behind to 'shoot' Baring.[42] He was forced to let them go, sick at heart.

At that moment, however, Baring heard the call 'victory, victory' erupt along the whole line, followed shortly after by 'advance, advance'. He probably did not know it yet, but his stubborn defence of the farmhouse had held up Napoleon for long enough to allow the arrival of Blücher. The allied centre had beaten off the French Imperial Guard. Tens of thousands of Prussians pressed in from the east and north-east. Napoleon's entire army was in full retreat.

Two battalions of Nassauers now advanced on La Haye Sainte, driving the last French defenders from its courtyard and gardens by dusk.[43] Ensign Frank emerged from under his bed on the first floor. The area around the farm was a scene of utter desolation, strewn with dead bodies. Edmund Wheatley, then still a captive, saw a cuirassier in a neighbouring field 'on his face with outstretched arms soaking in his blood. I never saw so gigantic a figure.' He reminded Wheatley 'of Goliath in ye Scriptures'. Shortly after, Wheatley came across an infantryman 'in a strange attitude. His head, his hands and knees, bent up to his chest, were forced into the mud and he looked like a frog thrusting itself into the slimy puddle.'[44] The scene would have been a far from static one, however, with stragglers heading in every direction, the badly wounded calling out, while those who could walk or hobble headed for safety. Jonathan Leach recalls 'the frightful carnage of men and horses lying in so comparatively small a compass [and] the groans and lamentations' of the injured.[45] Baring, for his part, no longer had any men under his command, and so he joined the 1st Hussar Regiment and pursued the enemy until the onset of darkness. The battle had been won.

Returning to the battlefield, Baring oversaw a melancholy roll-call.[46] 'Major Baring' – 'present'. 'Major Bösewiel' – 'dead'. 'Captain Holtzermann' – 'captured'. 'Captain Schaumann' – 'dead'. 'Lieutenant Kessler' – 'wounded'. 'Lieutenant Georg Meyer' – 'wounded'. 'Lieutenant Lindam' – 'wounded'. 'Lieutenant Christian Meyer' – 'present'. 'Lieutenant Rief-kugel' – 'wounded'. 'Lieutenant Tobin' – 'captured'. 'Lieutenant Carey' – 'wounded'. 'Lieutenant Biedermann' – 'present'. 'Lieutenant Graeme' – 'wounded'. 'Lieutenant Carl' – 'present'. 'Ensign von Robertson' – 'dead'. 'Ensign Frank' – 'injured'. 'Ensign Smith' – 'present'. 'Ensign Louis Baring' – 'present'. 'Lieutenant Timmann [adjutant]' – 'wounded'. 'Surgeon Heise' – 'present'.[47]

Of the nearly 400 men with whom he had begun the day, only forty-two remained with him at the end. Most of the rest were dispersed across the battlefield, dead, wounded or missing. It later transpired that most of the latter category survived the fight, but the full cost was still staggering for the time. Six sergeants, four corporals and twenty-one enlisted men were dead, including Rifleman Henry Busch, who had wed Harriet Haselden at Bexhill.[48] No fewer than twelve sergeants, sixteen corporals, one bugler and seventy-six enlisted men had been wounded. One sergeant, three corporals, two buglers and fifteen men were missing. Together with the officers, that made 168 casualties.

Overcome by conflicting emotions of anger and sorrow, Baring felt his eyes clouding over with tears. There was sadness at his dead and mutilated comrades, to be sure, and perhaps some survivor's guilt. But he also records his bitterness: probably at the failure to send adequate reinforcements or supplies of ammunition, the loss of so many good men and personal friends, the flight of his adjutant with the spare horses, and the men who had hesitated before coming to his aid from the sunken road. Conspicuously absent was any sense of triumph.[49] Wheatley too wondered whether it was all worth it. Shortly after the battle had ended he saw an infantryman leaning against a wall 'with his head back and both his eyeballs hanging on his cheeks, a ball having entered the side of his head and passed out the other'. 'His mouth', this lieutenant of the 5th Line Battalion King's German Legion recalls, 'was open, stiff and clotted, clear blood oozed out of his ears and the purulent matter from his empty sockets emitted a pale stream from the vital heat opposed to the evening cold'. 'So much for honour!' Wheatley reflected. 'Will it replace his orbs [eyes]? No.'[50] As night fell, thousands of such horrors must have been played out.

Baring was roused from his brooding by an old friend, Major Shaw, the divisional quartermaster-general. He was exhausted and in severe pain from his leg. The two men lay down to sleep on some straw. Lieutenant Biedermann, now reunited with the rest of the battalion, also settled in for the night 'between the mutilated corpses of friend and foe, a gruesome bedding-place'. In a moment of kindness, one of the cavalry sergeant-majors brought him some straw and covered him with a blanket.[51] A full moon now illuminated the battlefield whose 'profound stillness was disturbed only by the groans of the unfortunate wounded'. Their ordeal was by no means over, as those well enough to be moved faced the agony of a cart ride to hospital in Brussels. Many did not survive; how many further deaths the 2nd Light Battalion suffered the day after the battle and in the following weeks is not known, but must have been substantial.

The next morning Baring woke to find himself between a corpse and a dead horse, the sights and sounds of the previous day's carnage all around him. Biedermann too remembers the corpses, whose features had become 'distorted by blood and mud'. The Germans buried their dead officers, including the brigade commander, Ompteda. His body was found stripped. Around midday provisions finally arrived. The men of the 2nd Light Battalion sat around, like the dead their countenances marked with 'powder, filth and blood'. They used the various saddles, knapsacks, drums and other items strewn around the field as stools, the cavalry breastplates as frying-pans, and the capes of many a cuirassier 'who [only] yesterday had wanted to deprive us of the need to eat altogether' served as a tablecloth. After a modest meal and a short rest, what was left of the 2nd Light Battalion broke camp and set off in pursuit of the enemy.

7

'Heat and centre of the strife'

The defence of La Haye Sainte played a crucial part in the defeat of Napoleon. He came close to beating Wellington twice during the day. First of all, in the early afternoon, when d'Erlon's corps almost punched its way through the allied centre, but its left wing, which was assigned the critical task of securing the farmhouse and the crossroads behind it, was held up by Baring's men. Secondly, Napoleon almost prevailed in the early evening, when he was able to bring up artillery and reinforcements after the fall of the farmhouse.[1] Moreover, it must be remembered that La Haye Sainte was the principal focus of the French infantry between the rout of d'Erlon's men in the early afternoon and the final massed French attack on the allied centre several hours later. By the end, three of d'Erlon's four divisions were involved in the attack on the farmhouse. A large share of the French casualties were incurred in the vicinity of La Haye Sainte. In Donzelot's 2nd Infantry Division, the commander of the 2nd Brigade (Aulard) and of the 51st Ligne were both killed: the commanders of the 1st Battalion of the 51st Ligne, Pernet and Col Devienne were wounded. In Bourgeois's brigade of the 1st Infantry Division, commander of the 2nd Battalion 28th Ligne, Col Marrens, was mortally wounded, that of the 2nd Battalion 105th Ligne, Bonnet, was killed and the commander of the 105th Ligne, Gentry, was injured. In addition, the fighting for La Haye Sainte accounted for about 2,000 French casualties among the rank and file. La Haye Sainte was truly, as the poet Robert Southey put it, the 'heat and centre of the strife'.[2]

It is no coincidence, therefore, that Captain William Siborne's famous Waterloo panorama model of 1838 is timed at 7.45 p.m., the climax of the battle, not long after the failure to recapture the farm. If it had been taken earlier, then Napoleon would almost certainly have broken the allied centre, and defeated Wellington's army, before the Prussians had arrived in strength. The key mistakes made by both commanders concerned La Haye Sainte. Napoleon failed to devote enough thought and resources to its capture earlier in the day. Likewise, Wellington only woke up to the importance of the farmhouse when it was almost too late.

Baring did not win Waterloo on his own, of course: many others, including the defenders of Hougoumont, the Household Cavalry and not least Blücher, played a vital part in the battle; indeed, the British cavalry almost certainly saved the farm from capture in the early afternoon. Unlike the defence of Hougoumont, however, the struggle for La Haye Sainte and its environs was not merely 'a battle within a battle',[3] for much of the afternoon it *was* the battle.

Baring and his surviving men could look back at a considerable achievement. There had been fewer than 400 of them to start with, all soaked, hungry, exhausted and in some cases hung over even before the battle started. Even though the garrison was continually reinforced throughout the afternoon, it was at all times heavily outnumbered by the attackers. The men lacked the instruments to fortify the farm properly. From the early afternoon onwards, they were under more or less constant attack and subjected to frightening, if ineffective, shelling. Their shoulders were 'jellied' from the recoil of their weapons; their mouths 'begrimed with gunpowder'.[4] The combination of exertion, smoke, the biting off of cartridges and the earlier consumption of alcohol must have made them very thirsty. The sight of the dead and dying in confined spaces, and the plight of the wounded must have told on their nerves throughout. Nevertheless, the defenders held out for nearly five crucial hours while Napoleon's clock ticked. Men such as Friedrich Lindau and Ludwig Dahrendorf carried on even after suffering multiple wounds. Even as the farm was being overrun, the officers and men of the rearguard obeyed orders to hold the house, while the commander and the rest of the force escaped. The 2nd Light Battalion suffered something like 40 per cent casualties, close to the highest rate incurred by any formation at Waterloo, without disintegrating, although it began to wobble at the end.[5] Baring's men were thus, as Southey's poem put it, one of the 'rivets [in Wellington's line] which no human force could break'.

It is worth comparing their performance to that other link in Wellington's line: the château of Hougoumont. There was an important difference between the two experiences. The château never fell, not because the guardsmen were superior to the Legionnaires, but because the assault on it was never meant to be more than a diversion, even though it sucked in more and more of Reille's corps. The garrison, moreover, was never as hopelessly outnumbered as those at La Haye Sainte. In other respects, however, the two contests were remarkably similar. Both were international efforts – despite the salience of the guards, the Nassauers played a crucial role at Hougoumont. Above all, both confrontations unfolded in a closely defined space, which as John Keegan suggests, may have inspired a certain proprietorial territorialism among the defenders.[6] Finally, in both Hougoumont and La Haye Sainte, the garrisons suffered far higher casualties than regiments – such as the Lüneburgers, the 5th and the 8th King's German Legion Line battalions – which had been carved up by cavalry attacks before they could form square, and effectively ceased to take much more part in the battle thereafter.[7] This suggests that cohesion was determined not as much by casualty levels as by morale. If relatively few Lüneburgers were actually killed by the cuirassiers, the charge was so traumatic that the survivors lost the will to fight on. It was the delivery of moral rather than kinetic force which was decisive.

Why did Baring's men stand for so long? To address this question is to delve into the great mystery of courage in combat, which has been tackled by many scholars before,[8] and is especially elusive to a sedentary historian such as the present author. It would be tempting to attribute the resilience of the garrison to the existence of some sort of 'primary group' cohesion, a close relationship based on long common service (and often on similar geographical origins).[9] On such a reading, we are dealing with a close-knit group of men from the same area – Hanover – who had come through many campaigns fighting together side by side.

There are two problems with this interpretation. First, a substantial proportion of all Legionnaires were not

Hanoverians at all, but foreigners in the strict German meaning of the term. Secondly, while it is true that the men of the 2nd Light Battalion had a distinct record and pedigree, they were outnumbered in the farmhouse by other allied troops by the end of the siege. We know from the records that men from five other regiments were in the buildings: the 1st Light Battalion KGL, the light company of the 5th Line Battalion, stragglers from other companies of that battalion, some of the Lüneburgers who had escaped the initial French cavalry charge, and of course the Nassauers. It is also likely that some stragglers from the 8th Line Battalion made it to La Haye Sainte after being routed by cuirassiers. Moreover, a substantial proportion of the original 2nd Light Battalion garrison, including Lieutenant Biedermann, did not make it back to the farm after being charged by French cavalry at the start of the battle, and spent the rest of the day in one of the allied squares on the reverse slopes. In short, many of the men who fought on throughout the afternoon at La Haye Sainte can have had no personal prior connection, and in some cases did not even belong to the same army. Like countless soldiers across the ages, they continued to fight, forming and reforming around a dwindling cadre of surviving officers and NCOs.[10]

Nor were they held together by iron discipline, by fear of their superiors. It is well known that desertion was punishable by death, and we have many accounts of the men in squares and line being shoved back into line by their sergeants and beaten by officers with the flats of their swords, not out of callousness, but because a break in the ranks could spell death for all concerned. These methods did not apply at La Haye Sainte, however. The Legion still flogged, but it was known for its relatively light use of corporal punishment. Moreover, most of the garrison were light infantrymen of one sort or another and thus accustomed to being employed individually, out of sight of their officers. The kind of physical intimidation which officers and NCOs used on the battlefield in the line regiments was simply not feasible. Nor can it have been fear of stepping outside the relative safety of the buildings and being killed by the enemy. Admittedly, trying to escape by the field to the west, or by the road to the east, both of which were under constant enemy fire, and were crawling with cavalry and skirmishers to boot, would have been very hazardous. Most of the time, however, the farm was not completely cut off, and was connected to the main position through the kitchen garden, via which messengers left and reinforcements arrived. It would have been complicated, but by no means impossible, for individual members of the garrison to have slipped out this way. As far as we know, none did.

Ideological factors played a major role in boosting

combat cohesion. We have seen that many Legionnaires were united by a profound sense of German patriotism, and a determination to end Napoleonic tyranny.[11] This undoubtedly helped to sustain them throughout that long afternoon. Religious motivations, comparable to those in the sixteenth- and seventeenth-century European conflicts, do not seem to have weighed heavily with the Legionnaires. To be sure, Christianity – or versions of it – played an important role in the risings against French or British rule in Italy, Spain or Ireland in the Revolutionary and Napoleonic periods. It was not insignificant to British and Prussian opponents of Napoleon either.[12] It is also true that the Hanoverians – most of whom were Lutherans open to Anglican worship – indulged in all the conventional forms of piety, as their church attendance in Bexhill implies. Yet there is no suggestion that their stand at Waterloo was driven by any religious conviction.

The collective sanction of one's peers was surely more important. 'Honour' was a central concept not just for the officers but also for the rank and file.[13] All the accounts agree that it was an unwillingness to be seen to shirk which spurred the men on to greater efforts. The defenders were driven by a high degree of confidence in their leaders. The Duke was no doubt cold and calculating in many respects, but the fact is that he commanded the loyalty not only of his British troops, but also of the foreign troops under his command. There is no doubt that the officers of the King's German Legion enthusiastically reciprocated Wellington's high regard for them. The rank and file, in turn, believed in their officers, as their repeatedly professed willingness to fight on in the face of overwhelming odds attests. This obedience was not unconditional, however, but the result of an unspoken contract between officers and men that lives would not be needlessly sacrificed. There was always a moment when withdrawal or surrender became appropriate and honourable.[14] The moment close to the fall of the farm, when the rank and file assured Baring of their willingness to fight on *if* they were supplied with fresh ammunition was a subtle invocation of that understanding.

Finally, one should spare a thought for the French attackers who threw themselves repeatedly into the German rifle-fire. They too were mere flesh and blood, sometimes cowering behind a bank, sometimes white-faced and worn out, as the men who stormed the main buildings were even at the moment of their brief triumph. Yet they too showed incredible fortitude, from the captain of engineers who handed Octave Levavasseur his card before a hazardous charge to the pioneer sergeant who hacked at the main gate under a hail of bullets, and the nameless other thousands determined to capture the farmhouse. Unlike the Germans, who could at least tend to their wounded under cover, the French suffered where they fell, lacking even rudimentary dressing facilities, unless they were able to hobble back to the relative safety of their own lines. Not even mutilation could dampen the enthusiasm of some: reports speak of a wounded man screaming '*Vive l'empereur*' even as his limbs were being amputated. These men showed commitment and courage worthy of a better cause.

8

Legacy: A 'German Victory'?

In early February 1816, just under eight months after the battle, the King's German Legion was disbanded.[1] Many joined the army of the new Kingdom of Hanover, where they could continue to draw British half-pay. The British paymaster in Hanover, John Taylor, supervised this in person for another four years; in 1837, more than twenty years after the battle, there were still 158 half-pay officers in the Hanoverian army.[2] Others retired or went on half-pay. It fell to none other than George Baring, the hero of La Haye Sainte, to escort the flags of the Legion to their final resting place in the old Garrison Church of Hanover. There he spoke of his 'memory of joys and sufferings, the battles and the victories', which these banners had witnessed and of 'the loss of so many beloved comrades and of God's will by which alone he had survived so long'.[3] It is said that he was so moved by the event that he was scarcely able to articulate his final words of command as a Legionnaire. Perhaps he was thinking of the fatalities at La Haye Sainte and its environs, many of whom died unnecessarily, for want of ammunition, or – like Ompteda – in the execution of senseless orders.

The 2nd Light Battalion King's German Legion were hailed as heroes by contemporaries, as were all the Hanoverians who had served at Waterloo.[4] Ensign Frank, perhaps the luckiest member of the garrison, was commemorated with a plaque erected by his father in his home town of Fallersleben. The unfortunate Ensign Robertson was remembered in well-meant but excruciating verse published on the first anniversary of his death.[5] 'You too, the svelte youth, my Robertson,' the poetaster Dr Wilhelm Blumenhagen wrote, 'lie with bloodied head ... But you died well on the day of freedom, for the glory of your King and the salvation of your people. A bloody wreath will be a crown of palms.' Baring himself was ennobled in both Britain and Hanover – becoming both a baronet and a *Freiherr* – and rose to high rank in the army, eventually retiring as a lieutenant general. It took some time, though, before the collective contribution of the Legion was fully honoured. 'Should all these heroic events,' a correspondent of the *Hannoversches Magazin* lamented in April 1816, 'these deeds of heroic valour and pure patriotism remain completely unrecognized?'[6] 'For how long,' a piece in the same paper asked fourteen years later, 'must one yearn for a history of the English [*sic*] German Legion?'[7] It was only in the 1830s, some two decades after the battle, that their sacrifice was widely commemorated.[8]

In 1832, the Waterloo column in Hanover was completed. On it, the names of the Legionnaires were re-Germanized: Private George Heinz became Gottfried Heinz once more. That same year the first of the two volumes of Colonel North Ludlow Beamish's history of the Legion, which was eventually published in both English and German, appeared to great acclaim. When the second and final volume saw the light of day in 1837, grateful officers presented him with an elaborate silver centrepiece. This featured figures from a variety of KGL regiments, excluding the unfortunate 5th and 8th Line Battalions who had been routed by French cavalry at Waterloo. The 2nd Light Battalion was given pride of place at the very front, sharing the limelight with the 1st Hussar Regiment. The German oak at its core represented German liberty, which was being importuned by the French cockerel. Dispossessed Germania sits sobbing, while two German young men leave on a British ship. Britannia receives them and mobilizes them under the white horse of Hanover. Together with the British lion they confront and vanquish the cowering cockerel.[9] The whole crowded artefact was a poignant testimony to the extraordinary Anglo-German symbiosis which the Napoleonic threat had created, and the Legion epitomized.

The King's German Legion stayed largely aloof from the controversies which soon broke out between the British and Prussians about the battle. Its officers remained extraordinarily reluctant to criticize Wellington, and when in doubt defended him. If Baring resented the Duke's failure to send suitable ammunition or sufficient reinforcements, he certainly never said so publicly. All the same, the defensive tone of his subsequent reports of the engagement, both published and unpublished, showed an underlying feeling of grievance. There was certainly no sense of triumph, only sadness at the lives lost and bitterness at the behaviour of some. Given that the man directly responsible for the lack of rifle bullets, the brigade commander Ompteda, had died a hero's death, Baring's ability to complain was limited. Moreover, the divisional commander, Sir Charles von Alten, was a towering figure on the post-war Hanoverian scene who would have taken any public washing of dirty laundry very much amiss. Baring's reports also suggest that he was – needlessly – afraid of being accused of having given up the post too quickly. He was brave and intelligent, but no operator. Alten's account of the battle was bland to the point of colourlessness, while Baring waited too late to put pen to paper again, dying before he completed his autobiography, and crucially before reaching the events of

18 June 1815. In the end, while Baring was eventually commemorated in Hanover by a small plaque (actually Baring's own gravestone, which was transferred from his resting place in Wiesbaden in 1972), Charles von Alten was honoured with a large statue nearby, dwarfing that of his subordinate. He still stands guard in front of the Hanoverian state archive on the Waterlooplatz, which has now yielded up some but surely not all the secrets of what happened that afternoon.

For many of the rank and file the victory at Waterloo may have brought a large symbolic bounty, but the demobilization in 1816 brought fresh challenges. Many were too old for a new career. Others were broken in mind or body by the battle. Poor Rifleman Dahrendorf, for example, had a leg amputated. The provision for the demobbed enlisted men and their families was poor – they had to prove that any disabilities were service-related. That said, their officers did their best, with a stoppage of four days a year from their own pensions towards a special fund for widows and orphans of ex-Legionnaires who had fallen on hard times. This charity was administered by a committee of respected officers and remained in operation for many decades after the unit was disbanded; in the 1860s, it included an Oberstleutnant C. F. von Ompteda, a direct descendant of his Waterloo namesake.[10]

The officers, with their entitlement to half-pay, were better off, but they too were subject to demons. A number of Legion officers committed suicide, and many died before their time. Ensign Christian Göbel, formerly of the 5th Line Battalion, for example, 'shot himself in a fit of insanity' two days before the twelfth anniversary of the battle, possibly a delayed casualty of that terrible cuirassier charge. Four officers of the similarly brutalized 8th Line Battalion died in quick succession in 1817–18.[11] The survivors of the 2nd Light Battalion also suffered. Adjutant William Timmann, who had been seriously injured at La Haye Sainte, and may have been under something of a cloud for losing control of Baring's horses, probably never really recovered before his death at Hamburg in 1818. Lieutenant Georg Meyer, who had been slightly wounded defending the kitchen garden at La Haye Sainte, died on a Hanoverian army pension at Ottendorf in March 1823. Lieutenant Marius Tobin, who may have been of Dutch descent, breathed his last two years later in Surinam on the north-western coast of South America. Lieutenant Emanuel Biedermann, who had escaped hostile fire in La Haye Sainte, and hostile fire outside it, died in October 1836 at Steinhutte near Winterthur in his native Switzerland. It is not known – and perhaps not knowable – whether these untimely deaths were related to the traumas of that long afternoon.[12]

Most coped, one way or the other. Many of the 2nd Light Battalion's officers lived to a reasonable, and sometimes ripe old age. Lieutenant John Drummond Graeme, who had been slightly wounded at La Haye Sainte, where he formed such an inimitable duo with Rifleman Lindau, was still alive at Inchbraikie, Fife, Scotland in 1846. He still rejoiced in his nickname of 'Commander of the pigpen'.[13] George Baring was one of the first to go, garlanded with honours, dying at Wiesbaden in Hesse as a lieutenant general in the Hanoverian army in July 1848. Captain Ernst August Holtzermann outlived his brother Philip by more than thirty-seven years, dying a major-general in the North German town of Hamelin in 1852. Ensign George Frank, twice severely wounded at Waterloo, became a brevet captain on the Hanoverian army pension in 1816, and ended his days in August 1857 at Liebenberg, Hanover. Captain Ole Lindam, badly wounded at La Haye Sainte, was still living as a major on the Hanoverian retired list in Devonshire in 1865. Lieutenant Bernhard Riefkugel, who was also seriously injured at La Haye Sainte, died a major general at Hanover in December 1869.

Despite their experiences just outside the farm, some officers of the 5th Line Battalion involved with La Haye Sainte also enjoyed fulfilled later lives. Edmund Wheatley married Eliza Brooks in St Andrew-by-the-Wardrobe church in London, had three daughters and died in May 1841 at Trier in Western Germany. Lieutenant Charles von Witte, who had been sent into La Haye Sainte as part of the Light Company of the 5th Line Battalion, and wounded there, retired as a captain on a Hanoverian pension at the end of 1844. His company comrade, Lieutenant Charles Schläger, joined the new Hanoverian army as a captain in the Grenadier Guards and died a major. Ompteda's two nephews, Ludwig Albrecht and Christian Ludwig, happy to say, survived until 1860 and 1872, respectively. The intrepid battalion assistant surgeon, Georg Hartog Gerson, who had seen more ghastly sights than most, headed for Hamburg after the Legion was disbanded and rose to become the head surgeon of the Allgemeines Krankenhaus.

Even after its disbandment, the Legion remained an agent of cultural transfer from Britain to Germany; the traffic seems to have been largely one way. British mess customs were adopted in the Hanoverian army: there was to be no 'shop' spoken, and glasses had to be drained when drinking a toast. A passion for Georgian silver services was also imported from Britain. The new Hanoverian drill regulations drawn up by General von Alten followed the British model, the artillery used English weights and measures, the infantry was equipped with British rifles, and even such details as flogging routines were based on British practices. More generally, the Legionnaires brought back with them a predilection for all things English, especially the language and a desire to be perceived as a 'gentleman'. For many years yet, two veterans meeting each other in Germany would call out 'Old England Forever!'[14]

By the late nineteenth century, the Legion was regarded with more ambivalence in Germany, where historical memory was complicated by the unification project.[15] Hanover was invaded and annexed by Prussia in 1866. Simultaneously, nationalist unease about the service of Germans in foreign armies grew. The new German Empire after 1871 was anxious to subsume Hanoverian military traditions, and to repatriate the Legion from Britain.[16] Emperor Wilhelm II proved to be especially adept at this process of calculated amnesia, assimilation and appropriation; and in this particular case, his peculiar love–hate relationship with Britain may also have played a role.[17] In January 1899 he decreed that the traditions of the various old Hanoverian regiments, including the Legion, should pass to Prussian units with substantial numbers of Hanoverian recruits. Henceforth many of them carried the battle honours 'Peninsula-Waterloo'. Four years later, the Kaiser celebrated the hundredth anniversary of the founding of the Legion in 1803.

As the showdown with Britain loomed, the 'Germanization' of the Legion was intensified. The historian of the Legion Bernhard Schwertfeger even went as far as to claim, albeit in the shadow of war in February 1914, that it had been 'from its creation a purely Hanoverian unit under Hanoverian officers', a palpable untruth.[18] It was probably also for this reason that the Prussian historian Julius von Pflugk-Harttung's officially sanctioned printed source collection suppressed the lengthier and more candid of Baring's two official reports,[19] because it cast a bad light on the performance of certain regiments. The Vaterländische Museum in Hanover commissioned a diorama of the defence of La Haye Sainte, probably inspired by William Siborne's work.[20] However, the bicentenary of the personal union between Britain and Hanover in 1914 was swamped by the approach of the war. Some of the British and German units facing each other during that conflict carried the same battle honours from the Napoleonic wars.

The centenary of the battle itself in 1915 caused embarrassment to French, British and Germans alike, because the global conflagration united Britain to her former enemy, France, against her erstwhile ally, Prussia-Germany.[21] It cast a shadow over long-standing plans for an anniversary exhibition in Hanover. 'Our allies of that time,' the *Hannoverscher Kurier* noted sadly in June 1915, 'are today our sworn enemy.' When later generations of Britons 'compare[d], the accomplishments of the auxiliary peoples, whom they are employing against Germany in this war with the services that German armies rendered them a hundred years ago,' the same paper predicted bitterly, echoing the words attributed to the Roman emperor on hearing the loss of Varus's men in the Teutoberg Forest, 'it is only to be expected that they will one day send the baleful cry across the Channel: Germany, Germany, give me back your Legions!'[22]

After 1945, the Legion's boats did not rise with the general tide of enthusiasm for Germany's 'federal' traditions, partly because of unease about military heroism and partly because it was impossible to commemorate the battle without treading on the toes of the Federal Republic's new French partners. Indeed, a British attempt to send the Queen to place a wreath at the Waterloo column in Hanover during her acclaimed state visit to the Federal Republic in May 1965, almost 150 years after the events, was thwarted by the West German government.[23]

The French have generally been less interested in Waterloo. This was partly pique at a lost battle. Napoleon's officers, for example, spurned Siborne's requests for their testimonies when compiling his account of the events.[24] It also reflects that the wars took the French armies not only to the Peninsula and the Low Countries, but also to Germany, Italy, Russia and many other places besides, thus relativizing the importance of the final epic duel. The siege did not feature much in the post-battle French recriminations, which centred on Grouchy's absence and Ney's impetuousness. It is striking, though, that French accounts have tended to overestimate the size of the garrison, from Napoleon's preposterous suggestion of a division, to Jean Charras's much closer but still inflated figure of 430.[25] The only French memorial specifically relating to the farm-house was erected in 1965 during a small ceremony or-ganized by the Société belge d'études napoléoniennes and the cultural attaché at the French embassy in Brussels. It is dedicated simply: 'To the memory of the French combat-ants who sacrificed themselves heroically in front of the walls of La Haye Sainte on 18 June 1815'.

On the battlefield itself, the buildings still stand almost exactly as they did 200 years ago, well cared for and still a working farm. The landscape around it, however, has changed beyond recognition.[26] Immediately after the bat-tle, most of the deep ravines surrounding La Haye Sainte, in which French cavalry had lurked so fatefully, were filled in with dead bodies. Subsequently, the creation of the huge Butte de Lion mound in honour of the Prince of Orange, which now dominates the battlefield, involved such a mas-sive movement of earth that the contours of the ridge on either side of the farmhouse were completely altered. For example, the steepness which contemporaries described is no longer apparent. The battlefield, Victor Hugo charged, 'has been disfigured for its own glorification'; Wellington, on seeing the changes, is said to have exclaimed; 'They have ruined my battlefield.'[27] More recent road-widening works have further altered the character of the environs. None of this is made sufficiently clear to visitors. More generally, the on-site interpretation of La Haye Sainte leaves much to be desired. The panorama and museum do deal with the *The Hundred Days* defence of the farm-house, but give much greater prominence to Hougoumont, the cavalry charges and the attack of the Imperial Guard. A DVD account of the battle sold in the gift shop makes only brief mention of the King's German Legion, and none at all in connection with La Haye Sainte.[28]

In Britain, the legacy of La Haye Sainte and the Legion more generally has been very positive. Wellington's position, admittedly, was ambivalent. He paid handsome tribute to his allies in his immediate dispatch from the battlefield, but thereafter he tended to play down the German (especially Prussian) contribution.[29] In general, however, the British have been quick to acknowledge the military contributions of foreigners. Eighteenth-century heroes such as Prince Eugene of Savoy, who commanded in the War of the Spanish Succession, and Frederick the Great and Prince Karl Wilhelm Ferdinand of Brunswick, who commanded in the Seven Years War, were lionized by the public in their own time.[30] The famous *Waterloo Dispatch* painting by Sir David Wilkie clearly shows the Hanoverians alongside the usual assortment of Britons from across the United Kingdom. The Duke of Cambridge's General Order transferring the Legion to Hanoverian service in February 1816 spoke of it having been 'rendered immortal by the *combined* [author's italics] exertions of British and German valour'.[31] Even observers inclined to take a jaundiced view of most of the Duke's foreign auxiliaries, such as Johnny Kincaid – 'we were, take us all in all, a very bad army' – exempted the Legion. 'The British infantry and the King's German Legion,' he wrote, 'continued the inflexible supporters of their country's honour throughout, and their unshaken constancy under the most desperate circumstances showed that although they might be destroyed, they were not to be beaten.'[32] Likewise, Captain Leach wrote of his fellow-riflemen that 'Nothing could exceed the determined bravery with which the Germans defended the farmhouse of La Haye Sainte.'[33]

This respect is echoed in British popular culture today. Foreign soldiers in British service feature prominently in the famous *Sharpe* novels by Bernard Cornwell and their television adaptations. 'Sharpe's Waterloo', originally broadcast on ITV and widely sold in DVD, even includes scenes with Baring in the farmhouse. The commemorative plaque recently unveiled on the wall of the farmhouse by Major Gardner was a British, not a German initiative, executed by the Bexhill-based Hanoverian Study Group of which Gardner was chairman. There is also a plaque in the Memorial Gardens, Bexhill, which was unveiled by the Wellington biographer Lady Longford.

All the same, in Britain, the real significance of La Haye Sainte is still lost amid the (understandable) emphasis on the Guards at Hougoumont, the heavy cavalry charges, Picton's death, the resilience of the British infantry squares under artillery fire and cuirassier attack, and finally Maitland's *coup de grâce* to the Imperial Guard.

Was Waterloo a 'German victory'? This claim was first made by Julius von Pflugk-Harttung before and during the First World War, who argued that the campaign was 'a victory of Germanic strength over French impetuousness, in particular a success of the German people'.[34] It was later elaborated on by Peter Hofschröer in a series of important but controversial works. It has even found popular expression in the James Bond movie *The Living Daylights*. 'I should have known that you would take refuge behind that British vulture Wellington,' the villain General Bradley Whitaker reproaches the hero. 'You know he had to buy German mercenaries to beat Napoleon, don't you?' There is something in this interpretation. About 45 per cent of the men with whom Wellington *started* the battle spoke German of one sort or another, and the proportion increased with every Prussian formation reaching the scene. By the end, a clear majority of allied combatants were 'German'; to that extent Waterloo was indeed a 'German victory'.

It would be more accurate and more helpful, however, to describe Wellington's army as 'European': 36 per cent were British (that is English, Irish, Welsh and Scottish), 10 per cent were King's German Legion, 10 per cent were

Nassauers (who fought at both La Haye Sainte and Hougoumont), 8 per cent were Brunswickers, 17 per cent were Hanoverian regular army, 13 per cent were Dutch and 6 per cent 'Belgian' (Walloons and Flemings). This made Waterloo, in the recent words of the D-Day veteran and former British Chief of the Defence Staff Field-Marshal Edwin Lord Bramall, 'the first NATO operation'.[35] On this reading, Baring's men were a multinational unit, in a multinational army sent by an international coalition. Their divisional commander, von Alten, was aptly described by his biographer as a 'European soldier'.[36] In his final orders in February 1816, the Duke of Cambridge announced that at Waterloo the Legion had 'powerfully aided the cause of Europe' as well as of their sovereign, George III.[37] The King's German Legion, and especially Baring's 2nd Light Battalion, thus represents a German military tradition entirely distinct from that of the Austro-Prussian struggle for mastery, the *Kleinstaaterei* of the smaller principalities, the cumbersome *Reichesexekutionsarmee* of the old Holy Roman Empire, the Kaiser or the *Wehrmacht*.

Baring's achievement stands out in another respect. The heroism of the garrison of La Haye Sainte was rational, not suicidal; they fought to the last bullet, but not the last man. Ompteda's final charge may have been heroic, but one can regard it only with ambivalence today, because it led not only to his own death but to that of many men who followed his example. We would think even more of him had he stood his ground against von Alten and the Prince of Orange – easier said than done, of course – and refused to advance against his own better judgement. Baring by contrast did not recklessly sacrifice his men on a point of honour, or in a spirit of death-defying hubris. He held on as long as he reasonably could, and then withdrew on his own initiative. Most of the men under his command survived, although many suffered terrible wounds. He struck the right balance between completing the mission, the 'honour' of the battalion and the responsibility he bore towards his men. Baring's example is therefore the very opposite of the Thermopylae, or 'Stalingrad', complex in German military history, where soldiers sacrifice themselves in total, whether usefully or pointlessly. For more than fifty years the German army, the *Bundeswehr*, has wrestled with the problem of 'tradition', blind to the model before its eyes. Now it is time that Baring's achievement, and that of his men, is given the full recognition it deserves, especially by the Germans themselves.

None of this is to slight the role of the other protagonists, in particular the British and the Prussians, or for that matter the French. 'The greatness of those countries,' Victor Hugo writes, 'is in no way affected by the happening at Waterloo. Peoples are great, thank Heaven, irrespective of the grim chances of the sword. Neither England, nor Germany nor France can be contained in a scabbard.' Luckily we live in an age when the great western and central

European peoples have buried the hatchet. Their militaries work closely together through NATO and the day may not be far off when some of them join to form a single Union Army. If that happens, they could do worse than to turn to the King's German Legion for inspiration.

Appendices

The history book on the shelf is always repeating
itself

'Waterloo', Abba

Do we really need another book on Waterloo? After all, Wellington famously told posterity to 'leave the Battle of Waterloo as it is'. Fortunately, however, historians have not heeded him and none of the accounts since 1815, from William Siborne's pioneering work, through Jac Weller's exposition of the Duke's own perspective,[1] to John Keegan's vivid description of the sight, sound and smell of that day,[2] have left the battle quite as they found it. Of the many general accounts, the best are Alessandro Barbero's *The Battle*, a real work of art whose few faults should be seen not as blemishes, but as beauty spots which accentuate the perfection of the whole, and Mark Adkin's *Waterloo Companion*, a friend to whom one turns again and again for diversion and enlightenment.[3] The last two decades have also seen an increase in scholarship on the Personal Union between Great Britain and Hanover during the Napoleonic period, especially Torsten Riotte's *Hannover in der britischen Politik*, Christopher Thompson's work on the Hanoverian dimension in early nineteenth-century British politics, Peter Hofschröer's studies on the Hanoverian Army and the King's German Legion and Mark Wishon's pioneering work on the interaction between British and German military culture from the mid-eighteenth to the early nineteenth centuries.[4]

Despite this, the critical role played by the King's German Legion at Waterloo through their famous defence of the tactically vital farmhouse of La Haye Sainte has never been examined in sufficient detail. To be sure, the struggle for the farmhouse features prominently in every major account of the battle,[5] but always well behind the siege of the château of Hougoumont, the charge of the Union Brigade, Ney's cavalry attacks on the allied squares and the final futile advance of Napoleon's Imperial Guard.[6] Even revisionist works such as Peter Hofschröer's *The Waterloo Campaign. The German Victory*, which is largely focused on the Prussians, surprisingly devote only a few pages to La Haye Sainte.[7] Martin Mittelacher and Jochem Rudersdorf, who have done so much to highlight the contribution of troops from the German principality of Nassau to the defence of Hougoumont, and more generally at Waterloo, say little about the important contribution made by them at La Haye Sainte.[8] Jens Mastnak and Michael-Andreas Tänzer's comparatively recent account is full of interesting information and analysis, but is primarily designed as an accompaniment to an exhibition about the Hanoverian contribution to the battle as a whole, rather than as a detailed account of events in and around the farmhouse.[9] *La Haie-Sainte. Waterloo 1815* by Bernard Coppens and Patrice Courcelle is a battlefield guide full of interesting sources, and also makes a good case that Napoleon probably called the farm 'Mont-Saint-Jean', is essentially a collection of sources.[10]

FILM

The only major cinematic representation of the battle, Sergei Bondarchuk's artistically outstanding but historically somewhat suspect *Waterloo* (1970) (with Christopher Plummer as an unforgettable Wellington and Rod Steiger as an excellent Napoleon), makes no mention whatsoever of either Baring or the King's German Legion, despite Napoleon's *en passant* remark towards the end, 'the farmhouse is the key to the battle'.

NOTE ON TIMINGS

Establishing the exact *timing* of particular moments in the battle, and also of the siege of La Haye Sainte, is very difficult. For this reason, the author has generally avoided providing specifics and concentrated instead on establishing the *sequence* of events. Through a combination of source critique and cross-referencing it has been possible to do so with a considerable degree of accuracy. That said, it is possible that some of the cavalry charges on the KGL line regiments just outside the farm have been described in the wrong order, if for no other reason than that they appear to have been so jumbled by the participants themselves and later historians. Needless to say, in this as in all parts of the book, authorial error is not only possible but likely, and he would welcome any corrections.

In this connection, it is worth bearing in mind the injunction of Major Wilhelm von Schnehen written nine years after the battle: 'Everything that I am able to say about the battle of Waterloo can only be highly unsatisfactory and incomplete. From the moment that [my] regiment took active part in [the battle] the squadron under my command required my entire attention, so that a precise observation of what was going on far away from me was not possible. Some matters on which I might have been able to speak have escaped my memory after the passage of such along period of time.'[11] Nor should one forget the remarks of Christoph Heise: 'I know from experience [helping Beamish] what a difficult task it is to reconcile the contradictory reports of otherwise trustworthy and competent eyewitnesses, and to ascertain the true course of a

particular matter. Often the chronicler must simply be sat-
isfied that the opposing sides do not pounce on *him*.'[12]

NOTE ON SOURCES

In whatever degree we strive to become acquainted with
things past, and occupy ourselves with history in general,
yet we find at last that we gain most information from
the personal narratives of individuals, and the relation of
particular occurrences. On this account, therefore,
Memoirs, Auto-Biographies, Original letters, and Docu-
ments of this nature, are particularly sought after.

Johann Wolfgang Goethe, *Adventures of a Young Rifle-*
man in the French and English Armies during the War in
Spain and Portugal from 1806 to 1816 Written by Him-
self (2nd edn, London, 1826), p. 39 – memoir of a
Saxon-born rifleman in the King's German Legion.

This account is based on a wide range of sources, some of
them never previously used by historians of the battle.
There are many collections devoted to the battle as a
whole. The papers of William Siborne, who penned the
first serious analysis of Waterloo, are replete with eyewitness accounts from officers of the King's German Legion.[13]
The 'journals' of the regiments involved have been published by Julius von Pflugk-Harttung.[14] Gareth Glover has

done an excellent job in collecting and publishing sources, including those on the German side.[15] Thanks to the efforts of Andrew Field we now also have a picture of the French attackers not as an undifferentiated–Rorke's Drift-style mass – but (as far as the sources allow it) human flesh and blood.[16]

The sources hitherto un- or under-used by historians pertain more directly to La Haye Sainte. The commander of the 2nd Light Battalion, Major George Baring, wrote a detailed and well-known account in the 1830s, but a more revealing – and hitherto unused – report is to be found in the Hanoverian State Archive.[17] The papers of Colonel North Ludlow Beamish, by no means all of which found its way into his two-volume history of the Legion, also contain valuable material.[18] One of the junior officers of the Second Light Battalion, Lieutenant Biedermann, wrote a memoir. Most unusually for this period, we also have a very detailed description penned by Rifleman Lindau, a private soldier.[19] Moreover, because Hanover instituted the 'Guelphic Medal', to be awarded to non-commissioned officers and common soldiers, we have in the citations for valour a much fuller description of the activities of the rank and file than would otherwise be the case, albeit on the basis of recommendations by their superiors.[20] It goes without saying, of course, that eye-witness records need to be treated with caution.[21]

Bibliography

PRINTED PRIMARY SOURCES

Baring, Georg, 'Erzählung der Theilnahme des 2. Leichten Bataillons der Königlichen Deutschen Legion an der Schlacht von Waterloo', *Hannoversches Militärisches Journal* (2nd issue, Hanover, 1831)

de Bas, F. and de Wommersom, J. de T' Serclaes (eds.), *La Campaigne de 1815 aux Pays-Bas, d'après les rapports officiels néerlandais* (3 vols., Brussels, 1908–9)

Biedermann, Emanuel, *Erinnerungen, Wanderungen, Erfahrungen und Lebensansichten eines froh- und freisinnigen Schweizers* (2 vols., Trogen, 1828)

Brett-James, Antony (ed.), *Napoleon's Last Campaign from Eyewitness Accounts* (London, 1964)

Canler, Louis, *Mémoires de Canler, ancien chef du service de sûreté* (Brussels and Leipzig, 1862)

Cases, Emmanuel de las, *Mémorial de Sainte Hélène* (4 vols., Paris, 1823)

Chalfont, Alun Jones, Lord (ed.), *Waterloo: Battle of Three Armies* (London, 1979)

Clausewitz, Carl von, *On Wellington. A Critique of Waterloo*, translated and edited by Peter Hofschröer (Norman, OK, 2010)

Craan, W. R., *Plan du champ de bataille de Waterloo dit de La Belle-Alliance* (Brussels, 1816)

Dehnel, Heinrich, *Rückblicke auf meine Militär-Laufbahn 1805–1849 im KGL. Preussischen Heere, im Corps des Herzog von Braunschweig-Öls, im kgl. Grossbritannische. Und im Kgl. Hannov. Dienst* (Hanover, 1859)

———, *Erinnerungen deutscher Offiziere in britischen Diensten aus den Kriegsjahren 1805 bis 1816* (Hanover, 1864)

Drouet, Jean-Baptiste, comte d'Erlon, *Le Maréchal Drouet, comte d'Erlon. Vie militaire écrite par lui-même et dédiée à ses amis* (Paris, 1844)

Duthilt, Pierre-Charles, *Mémoires du capitaine Duthilt publiées par Camille Lévi* (Lille, 1909), extracts in *Bulletin de la Société Belge d'Études Napoléoniennes*, January 1955, 34–7, March 1967, 21–3

Fleuret, Dominique, *Description des passages de Dominique Fleuret, publiée par son petit-fils Fernand Fleuret* (Paris, 1829)

Glover, Gareth (ed.), *Letters from the Battle of Waterloo: Unpublished Correspondence by Allied Officers from the Siborne Papers* (London, 2004)

——— (ed.), *The Waterloo Archive: Previously Unpublished or Rare Journals and Letters Regarding the Waterloo Campaign and the Subsequent Occupation of France* (Barnsley, 2010)

Heinecke, Friedrich, *Meine Abenteuer als Werber gegen Napoleon, bearbeitet von Norbert Walter* (Hamburg, 1925) [written 1847]

Henegan, Sir Richard D., *Seven Years Campaigning in the Peninsula and the Netherlands 1808–1815* (2 vols., London, 1846)

Jacobi, Carl, *Erinnerungen aus dem Kriegsjahre 1815 und aus den Okkupationsjahren 1816, 1817, 1818. Ein Gedenkblatt für seine lieben Angehörigen von Carl Jacobi* (Hanover, 1865)

Kennedy, James Shaw, *Notes on the Battle of Waterloo* (London, 1865)

Kincaid, Captain Sir John, *Adventures in the Rifle Brigade in the Peninsula, France and the Netherlands from 1808 to 1815* (London, 1830, reprint Staplehurst, 1998)

Leach, Jonathan, *Rough Sketches of the Life of an Old Soldier* (London, 1831)

Levavasseur, Octave-René-Louis, *Un officier d'état-major sous le 1er Empire. Souvenirs militaires* (Paris, 1914)

Lindau, Friedrich, *Erinnerungen eines Soldaten aus den Feldzügen der Königlich Deutschen Legion* (Hamel-Hanover, 1846)

_____, *A Waterloo Hero. The Reminiscences of Friedrich Lindau*, edited and presented by James Bogle and Andrew Uffindell (London, 2009)

Mauduit, Hippolyte de, *Les Derniers jours de la grande armée ou souvenirs, documents et correspondance inédite de Napoléon en 1814 et 1815* (Paris, 2006)

Mercer, Cavalié, *Journal of the Waterloo Campaign, Kept throughout the Campaign of 1815*, by the late General Cavalié Mercer (Edinburgh and London, 1870)

Müffling, Friedrich Karl Ferdinand, Freiherr von, *History of the Campaign of 1815*, introductory observations and appendices by Sir John Sinclair, with a new introduction to the 1970 edition by B. P. Hughes (original published in German in 1815)

Napoleon's Memoirs, edited by Somerset de Chair (London, 1948)

Ompteda, Ludwig von (ed.), *Ein hannoversch-englischer Offizier vor hundert Jahren. Christian Friedrich Wilhelm Freiherr von Ompteda. Oberst und Brigadier in der Königlich Deutschen Legion. 26 November 1765 bis 18 Juni 1815* (Leipzig, 1892)

Puffahrt, Otto (ed.) *In der Schlacht von Waterloo gefallene, verwundete und vermisste Soldaten aus der Hannoverschen Armee* (Lüneburg, 2004)

Siborne, Herbert (ed.), *Waterloo Letters: A Selection from Original and Hitherto Unpublished Letters Bearing on the Operations of the 16th, 17th, and 18th June, 1815, by Officers who*

Served in the Campaign, edited, with explanatory notes, by H. T. Siborne (London, 1891)

Wellington, Arthur Wellesley, Duke of, *The Dispatches of Field Marshal the Duke of Wellington: During his Various Campaigns in India, Denmark, Portugal, Spain, the Low Countries, and France, from 1799 to 1818*, edited by John Gurwood (London, 1837–8)

————, *Supplementary Dispatches and Memoranda of Field Marshal Arthur, Duke of Wellington, K. G.*, edited by his son, the Duke of Wellington (15 vols., London, 1858–72)

————, *The Conversations of the First Duke of Wellington with George William Chad* (Cambridge, 1956)

————, *Wellington and His Friends: Letters from the First Duke of Wellington to the Rt. Hon. Charles and Mrs Arbuthnot . . .*, selected and edited by the Seventh Duke of Wellington (London, 1965)

Wheatley, Edmund, *The Wheatley Diary: A Journal and Sketchbook Kept during the Peninsular War and Waterloo Campaign*, edited by Christopher Hibbert (London, 1964)

Wissel, Ludwig von, *Ruhmwürdige Thaten, welche in den letzten Kriegen von Unteroffizieren und Soldaten der englisch-deutschen Legion und der Hannoverschen Armee verrichtet sind. Aus zuverlässigen Nachrichten zsgest. von Ludwig von Wissel* (Hanover, 1846)

SECONDARY SOURCES

Adkin, Mark, *The Waterloo Companion* (London, 2001)

Allgemeine Deutsche Biographie (56 vols., Leipzig, 1877–1912)

Andre-Dumont, Andre, 'Waterloo, 18 Juin 1815. Récit et essai d'explication' (unpublished mss, Brussels, 1968)

Angelow, Jürgen, '1815: Napoleons letzte Schlacht', *Militär und Geschichte: Bilder, Tatsachen, Hintergründe*, 43 (2009), 4–19

Barbero, Alessandro, *The Battle. A New History of Waterloo* (London, 2005)

Beamish, N. Ludlow, *History of the King's German Legion* (2 vols., London, 1832–7); German translation: *Geschichte der Königlich Deutschen Legion* (2 vols., 2nd edn, Berlin, 1906)

Bexhill Hanoverian Study Group, *From Bexhill to the Battle of Waterloo. A Story of the King's German Legion, 1804–1815* (Bexhill-on-Sea, 2003)

Black, Jeremy, *The Battle of Waterloo: A New History* (London, 2010)

Blanning, Tim, '18. Juni 1815: Waterloo', in Étienne François and Uwe Puschner (eds.), *Erinnerungstage. Wendepunkte der Geschichte von der Antike bis zur Gegenwart* (Munich, 2010), pp. 163–85

Bresemann, Manfred, 'The King's German Legion 1803–1816 and the British Traditions Handed down by the Legion to the Royal Hanoverian Army up to 1866', typescript in National Army Museum, NAM-355-453-3

Chandler, David, *Dictionary of the Napoleonic Wars* (London, 1979)

_____, *Waterloo. The Hundred Days* (Oxford, 1981)

Chappell, Mike, *The King's German Legion (I) 1803–1812* (Oxford, 2000)

_____, *The King's German Legion (II) 1812–16* (Oxford, 2000)

Charras, Jean, *Histoire de la campagne de 1815, Waterloo* (Brussels, 1857)

Chesney, Charles C., *Waterloo Lectures. A Study of the Campaign of 1815* (London, 1907)

Clark, C. M., 'The wars of liberation in Prussian memory: reflections on the memorialisation of war in early nineteenth-century Germany', *Journal of Modern History*, 68 (1996), 550–76

Coppens, Bernard (with Patrice Courcelle), *La Haie-Sainte, Waterloo 1815*, Les Carnets de la Campagne, 3 (2000)

Corrigan, Gordon, *Wellington. A Military Life* (London and New York, 2001)

Coss, Edward, *All for the King's Shilling. The British Soldier under Wellington, 1808–1814* (Norman, OK, 2010)

Cross, Edward J., 'Ordeal by fire: the combat behaviour of the British soldier under Wellington', *Proceedings of the Consortium on Revolutionary Europe*, 20 (1990), 681–9

Dallas, Gregor, *1815: The Roads to Waterloo* (London, 2001)

Dalton, Charles, *The Waterloo Roll Call* (London, 2nd edn, 1904)

Duchhardt, Heinz, von den Boer, Pim, and Schmale, Wolfgang (eds.), *Europaische Erinnerungsorte* (3 vols., Munich, 2012)

Dwyer, Philip, *Citizen Emperor. Napoleon in Power, 1799–1815* (London, 2013)

Epkenhans, Michael, Förster, Stig, and Hagemann, Karin (eds.), *Militärische Erinnerungskultur. Soldaten im Spiegel von Biographien und Selbstzeugnissen* (Paderborn, 2006)

Finkam, A., *Die an Baunschweiger und Hannoveraner verliehenen Ehrennzeichen* (Hanover, 1901, reprint Hamburg, 1974)

Förster, Stig, *The Battlefield: Towards a Modern History of War*, 2007 Annual Lecture, German Historical Institute (London, 2008)

Fraser, William Augustus, *Words on Wellington: The Duke–Waterloo–the Ball* (London, 1889)

Fremont-Barnes, Gregory, *Waterloo 1815* (Stroud, 2012)

_____ and Fisher, Todd, *The Napoleonic Wars. The Rise and Fall of an Empire* (Oxford, 2004)

Frevert, Ute (ed.), *Militär und Gesellschaft im 19. und 20. Jahrhundert* (Stuttgart, 1997)

Germain, Pierre, *Drouët d'Erlon, Maréchal de France* (Paris, 1985)

Gleig, George Robert, *Story of the Battle of Waterloo* (London, 1847)

Gray, Daniel S., 'The services of the King's German Legion in the army of the Duke of Wellington, 1809–1815' (DPhil dissertation, Florida State University, 1970)

Bibliography

_____, 'Prisoners, Wanderers, and Deserters': Recruiting for the King's German Legion 1803–1815', *Journal of the Society for Army Historical Research* (Autumn 1975), 148–58

Groote, Wolfgang von and Müller, Klaus-Jürgen (eds.), *Napoleon I. und das Militärwesen seiner Zeit* (Freiburg i. Br., 1968)

Guy, Alan J. (ed.), *The Road to Waterloo: The British Army and the Struggle against Revolutionary and Napoleonic France, 1793–1815* (Stroud and London, 1990)

Hagemann, Karen, *'Männlicher Muth und teutsche Ehre', Nation, Militär und Geschlecht zur Zeit der antinapoleonischen Kriege Preussens* (Paderborn, 2002)

Hamilton-Williams, David, *Waterloo: New Perspectives – The Great Battle Reappraised* (London, 1993)

Haythornthwaite, Philip J., *Waterloo Men. The Experience of Battle 16–18 June 1815* (Marlborough, 1999)

_____, *Wellington. The Iron Duke* (Washington, DC, 2007)

Heinzen, Jasper, 'Transnational affinities and invented traditions: the Napoleonic wars in British and Hanoverian memory', *English Historical Review*, 127 (2012)

Hibbert, Christopher, *Waterloo: Napoleon's Last Campaign* (New York, 2004)

Hofschröer, Peter, *The Hanoverian Army of the Napoleonic Wars* (London, 1989)

_____, 'Grant's Waterloo intelligence: was Dörnberg the cause of Wellington's delays?', *Journal of the Society for Army Historical Research*, 76 (1998), 163–76

_____, *1815. The Waterloo Campaign: Wellington, His German Allies, and the Battles of Ligny and Quatre Bras* (London, 1998)

_____, *1815. The Waterloo Campaign. The German Victory* (London, 1999)

Houssaye, Henry, *1815, Waterloo* (Paris, 1910)

Howarth, David, *Waterloo: A Near Run Thing* (London, 1968)

Hummel, Gisela and Carz, *Waterloo. Die hannoverschen Gefall-enen*, Welfenschriften 24 (Wedemark, 2006)

Hussey, John, 'Towards a better chronology for the Waterloo Campaign', *War in History*, 7 (2000) 4, 463–80

Keegan, John, *The Face of Battle* (London, 1976)

Kuhne, Thomas and Ziemann, Benjamin (eds.), *Was ist Militärg-eschichte?* (Paderborn, 2007)

Lanning, G. E., 'The King's German Legion in Dorset (1803–1805)', *Somerset Notes and Queries, Vol. XXXII*, March 1989, 749–56

Logie, Jacques, *Waterloo: l'évitable défaite* (Paris, 1984)

Longford, Elizabeth, *Wellington. The Years of the Sword* (London, 1969, 1971 paperback edn)

McNab, Chris (ed.), *Armies of the Napoleonic Wars. An Illustrated History* (Oxford, 2009)

Margerit, Robert, *Waterloo: 18. Juin 1815* (Paris, 1964)

Mastnak, Jens and Tänzer, Michael-Andreas, *'Diese denckwür-dige und mörderische Schlacht': Die Hannoveraner bei Water-loo; Begleitpublikation zur Grossdiorama-Ausstellung 'Die Schlacht von Waterloo' in der Ehrenhalle der Hannoverschen Armee im Bomann Museum Celle* (Celle, 2003)

Meissner, Hans-Reinhard, *Preussen und seine Armee. Von Valmy bis Waterloo* (Stuttgart, 2011)

Meulenaere, Philippe de, *Bibliographie analytique des témoignages oculaires imprimés de la Campagne de Waterloo en 1815* (Paris, 2004)

Mittelacher, Martin, 'Die Nassauer bei Waterloo: Aus der Sicht neuerer englisch-sprachiger Literatur', *Nassauische Annalen*, 109 (1998), 265–75

_____, 'Wellingtons Nassauer: Die Verteidiger der Domäne Hougoumont in der Schlacht bei Waterloo', *Nassauische Annalen*, 112 (2001), 329–48

Muir, Rory, *Tactics and the Experience of Battle in the Age of Napoleon* (New Haven, 1998)

_____, *Wellington. The Path to Victory, 1769–1814* (New Haven and London, 2013)

Naylor, John, *Waterloo* (New York, 1960)

North, Jonathan (ed.), *The Napoleon Options. Alternative Decisions of the Napoleonic Wars* (London, 2000)

North, René, *Regiments at Waterloo* (Edgware, 1971)

North, Roger, 'The raising and organising of the King's German Legion', *Journal of the Society for Army Historical Research*, 39 (1961), 168–84

Nosworthy, Brent, *With Musket, Cannon and Sword: Battle Tactics of Napoleon and his Enemies* (New York, 1996)

Nowosadtko, Jutta, *Krieg, Gewalund Ordnung. Einführung in die Militärgeschichte* (Tübingen, 2002)

Ompteda, Ludwig von, *Ein hannoversch-englischer Offizier vor hundert Jahren: Christian Friedrich Wilhelm Freiherr von Ompteda, Oberst und Brigadier in der Königlich Deutschen Legion. 26 November 1765 bis 18 Juni 1815* (Leipzig, 1892)

Paget, Julian and Saunders, Derek, *Hougoumont – The Key to Victory at Waterloo* (London, 1995)

Pelc, Ortwin, *Hamburg und Waterloo*, 29 (2000), Museum für Hamburgische Geschichte

Pelzer, Erich, 'Waterloo (18. Juni 1815): Schlachtenmythos und Erinnerungssymbolik', *Schlachtenmythen: Ereignis, Erzählung, Erinnerung*, edited by Gerd Krumeich (Cologne, 2003)

Pfannkuch, Adolf, *Die königlich deutsche Legion, 1803–1816 volkstümlich dargestellt von Adolf Pfannkuch* (2nd revised and expanded edn, Hanover, 1926)

Pflugk-Harttung, Julius von, *Vorgeschichte der Schlacht bei Belle-Alliance. Wellington* (Berlin, 1903)

_____, *Belle-Alliance* (Berlin, 1915)

_____, *Belle-Alliance (Verbündetes Heer). Berichte und Angaben über die Beteiligung deutscher Truppen der Armee Wellingtons an dem Gefechte bei Quatrebras und der Schlacht bei Belle-Alliance* (Berlin, 1915)

Platthaus, Andreas, 1813. *Die Völkerschlacht und das Ende der alten Welt* (Berlin, 2013)

Poten, Bernhard von, 'Georg Freiherr von Baring, Königlich Hannoverscher Generallieutenant: 1773–1848: Ein Lebensbild auf Grund von Aufzeichnungen des Verstorbenen und von Mittheilungen der Familie', *Militär-Wochenblatt* (1898) supplement

_____, 'Des Königs Deutsche Legion, 1803 bis 1816. Darstellung ihrer inneren Verhältnisse', *Militär-Wochenblatt*, supplement 11 (1905)

Quintin, Danielle and Bernard (eds), *Dictionnaire des colonels de Napoléon* (Paris, 1996)

Reinstorf, Ernst, 'Die bei Waterloo gefallenen Hannoveraner', *Zeitschrift für Niedersächische Familienleunde*, 21 (1939), 52–7

Richter, Klaus, 'Die Schlacht bei Waterloo: vor 190 Jahren wurde Napoleon endgültig besiegt', *Deutsche Militärzeitschrift*, 46 (2005), 50–54

Riley, J. P., *Napoleon and the World Wars of 1813. Lessons in Coalition Warfighting* (London and Portland, Oregon, 2000)

Riotte, Torsten, 'Die Entehung der Königlich-deutschen Legion (1803–1806). Hannoversche Truppen in britischen Diensten während der Napoleonischen Kriege' (MA, University of Cologne, 1999)

Roberts, Andrew, *Napoleon and Wellington* (London, 2001)

_____, *Waterloo: Napoleon's Last Gamble* (London, 2005)

Runnebaum, Julius, *General Karl von Alten: ein Soldat Europas* (Hildesheim, 1964)

Schmid, Josef Johannes (ed.), *Waterloo, 18. Juni 1815: Vorgeschichte, Verlauf und Folgen einer europäischen Schlacht* (Bonn, 2007)

Schnath, Georg, 'Die Legion Hanovrienne: eine unbekannte Hilfstruppe Napoleons 1803–1811', *Ausgewählte Beiträge zur Landesgeschichte Niedersachsens* (Hildesheim, 1968), pp. 280–329

Schwertfeger, Bernhard, *Geschichte der Königlich Deutschen Legion: 1803–1816* (2 vols., Hanover, 1907)

Shaw, Philip, *Waterloo and the Romantic Imagination* (Basingstoke, 2002)

Siborne, William, *History of the War in France and Belgium in 1815* (2 vols., London, 1844)

Strachan, Hew, *From Waterloo to Balaclava: Tactics, Technology, and the British Army, 1815–1854* (Cambridge, 1985)

_____ and Corum, Michael, *On the Fields of Glory: The Battlefields of the 1815 Campaign* (London and Stackpole, PA, 1996)

Uffindell, Andrew, 'Napoleon and Waterloo', in Jonathan North (ed.), *The Napoleon Options: Alternative Decisions of the Napoleonic Wars* (London, 2000)

_____, *Waterloo Commanders: Napoleon, Wellington and Blücher* (Barnsley, 2007)

Vigors, D. D., *The Hanoverian Guelphic Medal of 1815: A Record of Hanoverian Bravery during the Napoleonic Wars* (Salisbury, 1981)

Wacker, Peter and Muller-Schellenberg, Guntram, *Das herzoglich-nassauische Militär 1813–1866* (Taunusstein, 1998)

Weigley, Russell F., *The Age of Battles: The Quest for Decisive Warfare from Breitenfeld to Waterloo* (London, 1993)

Weller, Jac, *Wellington at Waterloo* (London, 1967)

Wette, Wolfram (ed.), *Der Krieg des kleinen Mannes. Eine Militärgeschichte von unten* (Munich, 1992)

Notes

PREFACE

1. See generally, Tim Blanning, '18. Juni 1815: Waterloo', in Étienne François and Uwe Puschner (eds.), *Erinnerungstage. Wendepunkte der Geschichte von der Antike bis zur Gegenwart* (Munich, 2010), pp. 163–85.
2. Rowena Mason, 'Waterloo battlefield in Belgium to get £1 million for 200th anniversary', *Daily Telegraph*, 26.6.2013.
3. Ben Macintyre, 'Without Prussia we'd all be speaking French', *The Times*, 28.6.2013.
4. Quoted in Albert A. Nofi, *The Waterloo Campaign, June 1815* (Cambridge, MA, 1998), p. 29.
5. *Childe Harold's Pilgrimage*, Canto the Third, stanzas 18 and 35.

I. PRELUDE

1. For a detailed account see Peter Hofschröer, *1815. The Waterloo Campaign: Wellington, his German Allies and the Battles of Ligny and Quatre Bras* (London, 1998) and Peter Hofschröer, *Waterloo 1815. Quatre Bras and Ligny* (Barnsley, 2005).

2. Friedrich Lindau, *A Waterloo Hero. The Reminiscences of Friedrich Lindau*, edited and presented by James Bogle and Andrew Uffindell (London, 2009), pp. 160–61.

3. Emanuel Biedermann, *Erinnerungen, Wanderungen, Erfahrungen und Lebensansichten eines froh- und freisinnigen Schweizers* (2 vols., Trogen, 1828), vol. 1, p. 187.

4. David Miller, *The Duchess of Richmond's Ball, 15 June 1815* (Staplehurst, 2005), pp. 120–21, tells us that only one KGL officer, belonging to another brigade, was present.

5. John Kincaid, *Adventures in the Rifle Brigade in the Peninsula, France and the Netherlands from 1808 to 1815* (London, 1830, reprint Staplehurst, 1998), pp. 160–62.

6. Biedermann, *Erinnerungen*, vol. 1, pp. 185–7.

7. Ibid., p. 186.

8. Wellington to Earl Bathurst, 19.6.1815, *Wellington Historical Documents: 1783–1832*, edited by A. Aspinall and E. A. Smith. Front cover. David Charles Douglas (Oxford, 1959), p. 933.

9. Biedermann, *Erinnerungen*, vol. 1, p. 186.

10. Private information from the owner, Count François Cornet d'Elzius.

11. I am following here the chronology of ibid. p. 188.

12. Thus Carole Divall, 'To the last cartridge. Wilhelm Wiese and Simon Lehmann of the King's German Legion', in idem, *Napoleonic Lives. Researching the British Soldiers of the Napleonic Wars* (Barnsley, 2012), p. 81.

13. David Howarth, *Waterloo: A Near Run Thing* (London, 1968), p. 121.

14. Biedermann, *Erinnerungen*, vol. 1, p. 189.

15. For an evocative account of the French army see Alan Forrest, *Napoleon's Men. The Soldiers of the Revolution and Empire* (London and New York, 2002).

16. Louis Canler, *Mémoires de Canler, ancien chef du service de sûreté* (Brussels and Leipzig, 1862), pp. 10–11.

17. Jean-Baptiste Drouet, Comte d'Erlon, *Le Maréchal Drouet, Comte d'Erlon. Vie militaire écritr par lui-même et dédieé à ses amis* (Paris, 1844), p. 96.
18. Canler, *Mémoires*, pp. 10–12.
19. D'Erlon, *Vie militaire*, p. 96.
20. Biedermann, *Erinnerungen*, vol. 1, p. 189.

2. FOR KING AND FATHERLAND

1. The numbers of the 2nd Light Battalion fluctuated – reaching a peak of 695 in October 1810 – but were normally about 460 men. They were thus seriously under strength at Waterloo: 'Monthly returns of Quarters of H. M. troops as applicable to Bexhill from 1795–1819' (figures for 1804–14), Bexhill Hanoverian Study Group Records.
2. See N. Ludlow Beamish, *History of the King's German Legion* (2 vols., London, 1832–7); N. Ludlow Beamish, *Geschichte der Königlich Deutschen Legion* (2 vols., 2nd edn, Berlin, 1906) (German translation with some additional material); Bernhard Schwertfeger, *Geschichte der Königlich Deutschen Legion, 1803–1816* (2 vols., Hanover, 1907); Mike Chappell, *The King's German Legion (I) 1803–1812* (Oxford, 2000). The KGL is not to be confused with the Hanoverian army itself, which was later reconstituted and also fought at Waterloo: Peter Hofschröer (text) and Bryan Fosten (colour plates), *The Hanoverian Army of the Napoleonic Wars* (Oxford, 1989).
3. For the earlier period see Torsten Riotte, 'Die Entstehung der Königlich-deutschen Legion (1803–1806). Hannoverschen Truppen in britischen Diensten während der Napoleonischen Kriege' (MA, University of Cologne, 1999), and for the later period Daniel S. Gray, 'The services of the King's German Legion in the Army of the Duke of Wellington, 1809–1815' (DPhil dissertation, Florida State University, 1970), and 'Chronologische Übersicht der K. deutschen Legion besonders

mit Bezug auf die leichten Infanterie batallions vom Jahre 1805 bis 1816', by Major Rautenberg, 1st Light Battalion, KGL, Hauptsstaatsarchiv Hannover (hereafter HStAH), Hann38D, 234. The definitive account for the whole period is Jens Mastnak, 'Werbung und Ersatzwesen der Königlich Deutschen Legion 1803–1813', *Militärgeschichtliche Zeitschrift* 60 (2001), 119–42, and his forthcoming *Die King's German Legion 1803–1816. Lebenswirklichkeit in einer militärischen Formation der Koalitionskriege.* The broader context is provided by Mark Wishon, *German Forces and the British Army. Interactions and Perceptions, 1742–1815* (Basingstoke, 2013), pp. 165–92.

4. 'Proposals for enlisting recruits from amongst prisoners of war in England for the King's German Legion', Horse Guards, 17.10.1811, in Bexhill Hanoverian Study Group, *Newsletter* 44 (November 2005).

5. As extrapolated from Otto Puffahrt (ed.), *In der Schlacht von Waterloo gefallene, verwundete und vermisste Soldaten aus der Hannoverschen Armee* (Lüneburg, 2004), pp. 70–77. We do not know more about the replacements for the 2nd Light Battalion because all papers were lost on board HMS *Northumberland* when it went down in the Irish Sea in 1807 (Bernhard Schwertfeger, *Peninsula-Waterloo. Zum Gedächtnis der königlich-deutschen Legion* (Hanover, 1914), p. 211.

6. See the figures in Jens Mastnak, 'Die Königlich Deutsche Legion, 1803–1816. Lebenswirklichkeit in einer militärischen Formation der Koalitionskriege' (PhD dissertation, University of Vechta, 2012), p. 121.

7. See Terry Cooper, 'Officers of the King's German Legion, 1803–1816', typescript, York, 1999, which updates and consolidates Beamish and Schwertfeger, pp. 18, 24, 25, 30, 36–7 (for British paymasters). Typescript in National Army Museum, NAM-1999-03-138-1-1, and Peter B. Boyden, 'The King's German Legion and their bankers', typescript in records of Bexhill Hanoverian Study Group.

8. For an evocative account see Mark Urban, *Rifles. Six Years with Wellington's Legendary Sharpshooters* (London, 2003).

9. For conditions of service see Beamish, *King's German Legion*, vol. 1, p. 350.

10. Bernhard von Poten, 'Des Königs Deutsche Legion, 1803 bis 1816. Darstelling ihrer inneren Verhältnisse', *Militär-Wochenblatt*, supplement, 11 (1905), 397–458 (quotation 421).

11. Thus Emanuel Biedermann, *Erinnerungen, Wanderungen, Erfahrungen und Lebensansichten eines froh- und freisinnigen Schweizers* (2 vols., Trogen, 1828) vol. 1, p. 141. For a detailed discussion of this see Jens Mastnak, 'Die Königlich Deutschen Legion, 1803–1816. Lebenswirklichkeit in einer militärischen Formation der Koalitionskriege' (PhD dissertation, University of Vechta, 2012), pp. 182–205.

12. See Julius Runnebaum, *General Karl von Alten: ein Soldat Europas* (Hildesheim, 1964).

13. For Wellington and the King's German Legion in the Peninsula and Southern France see Huw J. Davies, *Wellington's Wars. The Making of a Military Genius* (New Haven and London, 2012), pp. 105, 165, 200; Lawrence James, *The Iron Duke. A Military Biography of Wellington* (London, 1992), pp. 137–9. Michael Glover, *Wellington as Military Commander* (London, 1968), pp. 132 and 177.

14. Poten, 'Des Königs Deutsche Legion', p. 421.

15. Ibid.

16. 'Journale der Acht Linien und Veteranen Batallione der King's German Legion, 1803 bis 1816', HStAH, Hann38D, 236, fol. 225.

17. Jasper Heinzen and Mark Wishon, '"A patriotic mercenary?" Sir Julius von Hartmann as a Hanoverian officer in British service, 1803–1816', *Comparativ: Zeitschrift für Globalgeschichte und vergleichende Gesellschaftsforschung*, 23:2 (2013), 13–26. I thank Jasper Heinzen for letting me see this text in advance of publication. See also J. von Hartmann

(Jnr), *Der Königlich-Hannoversche General Sir Julius von Hartmann. Eine Lebensskizze* (Hanover, 1858).

18. Bexhill Museum Local History Folder A/HF20 (list of marriages).
19. See Brendan Simms, *Three Victories and a Defeat. The Rise and Fall of the First British Empire, 1714–1783* (London, 2007), pp. 417–18 *et passim*.
20. See Nicholas B. Harding, 'Hanover and British republicanism', in Brendan Simms and Torsten Riotte (eds.), *The Hanoverian Dimension in British History, 1714–1837* (Cambridge, 2007), pp. 301–23 (especially 32–22).
21. Bernhard von Poten, 'Georg Freiherr von Baring, Königlich Hannoverscher Generallieutenant: 1773–1848: Ein Lebensbild auf Grund von Aufzeichnungen des Verstorbenen und von Mittheilungen der Familie', *Militär-Wochenblatt*, 1 (1898), 1–78, here 35. See also Janet Harris, 'The KGL at Bexhill on Sea', in Gwen Davis (ed.), *The King's German Legion. Records and Research* (Anglo-German Family History Society Publications, Maidenhead, 2000), pp. 12–17, especially pp. 13–14.
22. A list has been compiled by Dr Vernon of the Bexhill Hanoverian Study Group: 'The King's German Legion, marriages 1804–1814', St Peter's Church, Bexhill-on-Sea, Sussex.
23. See 'KGL marriages, 1804–1814, St Peter's Church, Bexhill' after Dr Vernon of Bexhill with additional information from Terry Cooper of York, Archives of the Bexhill Hanoverian Study Group, Bexhill Old Town Preservation Society.
24. For a discussion of the complex motivations see Heinzen and Wishon, '"A patriotic mercenary?"', quotation p. 18, and Mastnak, 'Die Königlich Deutsche Legion, 1803–1816', pp. 141–6, which emphasizes non-pecuniary and patriotic motivations, but cautions against anachronistic assumptions of national feeling.
25. See Schwertfeger, *Peninsula-Waterloo*, p. 26.

26. A comparison made by David Howarth, *Waterloo: A Near Run Thing* (London, 1968), p. 119.

27. Quoted in Heinzen and Wishon, ' "A patriotic mercenary?" ', p. 18. For Hanoverians serving with Napoleon see Georg Schnath, 'Die Legion Hanovrienne. Eine unbekannte Hilfstruppe Napoleons 1803–1811', in Georg Schnath, *Ausgewählte Beiträge zur Landesgeschichte Niedersachsens* (Hildesheim, 1968), pp. 280–329.

28. Friedrich Heinecke, *Meine Abenteuer als Werber gegen Napoleon bearbeitet von Norbert Walter* (Hamburg, 1925) (originally written in 1847), pp. 5–6. For a broader look at such sentiments in North Germany see Karen Hagemann, 'Francophobia and patriotism: anti-French images and sentiments in Prussia and Northern Germany during the anti-Napoleonic wars', *French History*, 18, 4 (2004), 404–25.

29. Anonymous, *Erinnerungen eines Legionärs oder Nachrichten von den Zügen der Deutschen Legion des Königs (von England) in England, Irland, Dänemark, der Pyrenäischen Halbinsel, Malta, Sicilien und Italien. In Auszügen aus dem vollständigen Tagebuche eines Gefährten derselben* (Hanover, 1826), p. 1.

30. In Lindau, *A Waterloo Hero*, p. 22; see also p. 25.

31. Biedermann, *Erinnerungen*, vol. 1, pp. 71, 146–7.

32. Edmund Wheatley, *The Wheatley Diary. A Journal and Sketchbook Kept during the Peninsular War and the Waterloo Campaign*, edited with an introduction and notes by Christopher Hibbert (London, 1964), p. 64.

33. For how this fitted into the long-standing 'British way of warfare', see Wishon, *German Forces and the British Army*, p. 2 *et passim*. The phrase comes from David French, *The British Way of Warfare, 1688–2000* (London, 1990).

34. See See A. Hirsch, 'Georg Hartog Gerson', *Allgemeine Deutsche Biographie* 9 (Leipzig, 1879), pp. 57–9; Ortwin Pelc, *Hamburg und Waterloo*, Museum für Hamburgische Geschichte, 29 (2000); and Georg Baumann, 'Dr Georg

Hartog Gerson', Bexhill Hanoverian Study Group, Newsletter 49 (April 2008).

35. See Brendan Simms, *The Impact of Napoleon. Prussian High Politics, Foreign Policy and the Crisis of the Executive, 1797–1806* (Cambridge, 1997), p. 238' and F. von Ompteda (ed.), *Politischer Nachlass des hannoverschen Staats- und Cabinetsministers, Ludwig von Ompteda aus den Jahren 1804 bis 1813* (Jena, 1869).

36. Ludwig von Ompteda (ed.), *Ein hannoversch-englischer Offizier vor hundert Jahren: Christian Friedrich Wilhelm Freiherr von Ompteda. Oberst und Brigadier in der Königlich Deutschen Legion. 26 November 1765 bis 18 Juni 1815* (Leipzig, 1892), pp. 270–71.

37. Christian von Ompteda to Ludwig von Ompteda, 8.6.1815, Écaussines-Lalaing, near Soignies and Braine le Comte, Ompteda, *Ein hannoversch-englischer Offizier,* p. 272.

38. Ibid., p. 274.

39. Thus Baring's own autobiographical account: Poten, 'Georg Freiherr von Baring', p. 8.

40. Ibid. p. 9.

3. A TRAGEDY OF ERRORS

1. Jac Weller, *Wellington at Waterloo* (London, 1967).

2. Thus the composite narrator in Ludwig von Ompteda (ed.) *Ein hannoversch-englischer Offizier vor hundert Jahren: Christian Friedrich Wilhelm Freiherr von Ompteda. Oberst and Brigadier in der Königlich Deutschen Legion. 26 November 1765 bis 18 Juni 1815* (Leipzig, 1892)' p. 280.

3. Heinrich Dehnel, *Erinnerungen deutscher Offiziere in britischen Diensten aus den Kriegsjahren 1805 bis 1816* (Hanover, 1864), pp. 285–6.

4. Friedrich Lindau, *A Waterloo Hero. The Reminiscences of Friedrich Lindau,* edited and presented by James Bogle and Andrew Uffindell (London, 2009), p. 163.

5. Emanuel Biedermann, *Erinnerungen, Wanderungen, Erfahrungen und Lebensansichten eines froh- und freisinnigen Schweizers* (2 vols., Trogen, 1828), vol. 1, p. 190.
6. As shown in the Ground Plan of La Haye Sainte, HStAH, Hann8D, 243, fol. 211.
7. Lindau, *A Waterloo Hero*, p. 163.
8. Quoted in Alessandro Barbero, *The Battle. A New History of Waterloo* (London, 2005), p. 152.
9. John Kincaid, *Adventures in the Rifle Brigade, in the Peninsula, France and the Netherlands from 1808 to 1815* (London, 1830, reprint Staplehurst, 1998).
10. See Ian Fletcher, *A Desperate Business. Wellington, the British Army and the Waterloo Campaign* (Staplehurst, 2001), pp. 99–100.
11. See Dehnel, *Erinnerungen deutscher Offiziere*, p. 286; Ompteda, *Ein hannoversch-englischer Offizier*, p. 281; Jonathan Leach, *Rough Sketches of the Life of an Old Soldier* (London, 1831), p. 383.
12. Edmund Wheatley, *The Wheatley Diary. A Journal and Sketchbook Kept during the Peninsular War and the Waterloo Campaign*, edited with an introduction and notes by Chtistopher Hibbert (London, 1964), p. 63.
13. 'Effectiver Bestand des vormaligen 2ten Leichten Batalions der K. D. Legion in der Schlacht von Waterloo', by Lt B. Riefkugel, 20.11.1824, HStAH, Hann41, 152, fol. 45.
14. Not under Baring's command, as he was junior to Busche. See 'Wyneken remarks to Waterloo', HStAH, Hann 38D, 243, fol. 47. The company commanders were Wyneken and von Goeben.
15. Thus Baron Ernst vom Knesebeck, Travellers Club, 27.7.1845, in Gareth Glover (ed.), *Letters from the Battle of Waterloo: Unpublished Correspondence by Allied Officers from the Siborne Papers* (London, 2004), p. 306.
16. Barbero, *The Battle*, p. 63.

17. Louis Canler, *Mémoires de Canler, ancien chef du service de sûreté* (Brussels and Leipzig, 1862), p. 12
18. Ibid., pp. 13–14.
19. Quoted in Andrew W. Field, *Waterloo. The French Perspective* (Barnsley, 2012), p. 51.
20. Jean Charras, *Histoire de la campagne de 1815, Waterloo* (Brussels, 1857), p. 255.
21. See Field, *Waterloo. The French Perspective*, p. 57.
22. Barbero, *The Battle*, pp. 72–3.
23. See Bernard Coppens and Patrice Courcelle, *La Haie-Sainte, Waterloo 1815*, Les Carnets de la Campagne, 3 (2000) on this issue. See also Glenn van den Bosch, 'The importance of maps at the battle of Waterloo', *Brussels International Map Collectors' Circle*, May 2008, 15–17.
24. Field, *Waterloo. The French Perspective*, p. 57.
25. Jean-Baptiste Drouet, comte d'Erlon, *Le Maréchal Drouet, comte d'Erlon. Vie militaire écrite par lui-même et dédieé à ses amis* (Paris, 1844), p. 97.
26. See Barbero, *The Battle*, p. 153.

4. BOLTING THE BARN DOOR

1. Gareth Glover (ed.), *The Waterloo Archive. Volume II: German Sources* (Barnsley, 2010), p. 135.
2. Mark Adkin, *The Waterloo Companion* (London, 2001), p. 298.
3. Quoted in Alessandro Barbero, *The Battle. A New History of Waterloo* (London, 2005), p. 130.
4. Heinrich Dehnel, *Erinnerungen deutscher Offiziere in britischen Diensten aus den Kriegsjahren 1805 bis 1816* (Hanover, 1864), p. 287.
5. N. Ludlow Beamish, *Geschichte der Königlich Deutschen Legion* (2 vols., Berlin, 1906), vol. 2, p. 381.
6. See the description by Edward Cotton, *A Voice from Waterloo* (London, 1974, first published 1849), p. 32, and that of Jon-

athan Leach, *Rough Sketches of the Life of an Old Soldier* (London, 1831), p. 387, who was positioned just beside the farm.

7. Quoted in Gareth Glover (ed.), *The Waterloo Archive. Vol. IV: British Sources* (Barnsley, 2012), p. 217.

8. John Kincaid, *Adventures in the Rifle Brigade in the Peninsula, France and the Netherlands from 1808 to 1815* (London, 1830, reprint Staplehurst, 1998), p. 164.

9. As described in Emanuel Biedermann, *Erinnerungen, Wanderungen, Erfahrungen and Lebensansichten eines froh- and freisinnigen Schweizers* (2 vols., Trogen, 1828), vol. 1, p. 190.

10. Thus ibid., pp. 190–91.

11. For a perfectly plausible alternative view see David Buttery, *Waterloo. Battlefield Guide* (Barnsley, 2013), pp. 81–4 (with map on p. 80).

12. See Adkin, *The Waterloo Companion*, p. 343.

13. Louis Canler, *Mémoires de Canler, ancien chef du service de sûreté* (Brussels and Leipzig, 1862), p. 13.

14. Ibid.

15. Cotton, *A Voice from Waterloo*, p. 53.

16. Leach, *Rough Sketches*, p. 387.

17. John Kincaid, *Adventures in the Rifle Brigade and Random Shots from a Rifleman* (London, 1835, this edition London, 1981), pp. 165–6.

18. Quoted in Friedrich Lindau, *A Waterloo Hero. The Reminiscences of Friedrich Lindau*, edited and presented by James Bogle and Andrew Uffindell (London, 2009), p. 167.

19. See Hippolyte de Mauduit, *Les Derniers jours de la grande armée ou sourenirs, documents et correspondance inédite de Napoléon en 1814 et 1815* (Paris, 1848), pp. 333–4.

20. There is an evocative account in Adkin, *Waterloo Companion*, p. 166.

21. See Philip Elliot-Wright, *Rifleman. Elite Soldiers of the Wars against Napoleon* (London, 2000), pp. 73–81.

22. See Bernhard von Poten, 'Georg Freiherr von Baring, Königlich Hannoverscher Generallieutenant: 1773–1848. Ein Lebensbild auf Grund von Aufzeichnungen des Verstorbenen und von Mittheilungen der Familie', *Militär Wochenblatt* 55, and E. Grosse and Franz Otto, *Waterloo. Gedenkbuch an das glorreiche Jahr 1815* (Leipzig, 1865), p. 54.

23. Ludwig von Wissel, *Ruhmwürdige Thaten, welche in den letzten Kriegen von Unteroffizieren und Soldaten der englisch-deutschen Legion und der hannoverschen Armee verrichtet sind. Aus zuverlässigen Nachrichten zsgest. von Ludwig von Wissel* (Hanover, 1846), p. 130.

24. Thus the eyewitness account of Leach, *Rough Sketches*, p. 387 and Kincaid, *Adventures in the Rifle Brigade*, p. 166.

25. Bernhard Schwertfeger, *Geschichte der Königlich Deutschen Legion, 1803–1816* (2 vols., Hanover, 1907) vol. 1, pp. 605–6.

26. Christoph Heise to Captain Benne, 4.12.1840, in Gareth Glover (ed.), *Letters from the Battle of Waterloo: Unpublished Correspondence by Allied Officers from the Siborne Papers* (London, 2004), p. 231.

27. Account of Captain Frederick von Gilsa, Eimbeck, 9.12.1840, in ibid., pp. 225–6.

28. See N. Ludlow Beamish, *History of the King's German Legion* (2 vols., London, 1832–7), vol. 2, p. 512.

29. Christoph Heise to Captain Benne, 4.12.1840, in Glover (ed.), *Letters from the Battle of Waterloo*, pp. 231–2. On Sander see Adolf Pfannkuch, *Die königlich deutsche Legion, 1803–1816* (Hanover, 1926), p. 243.

30. See Poten, 'Georg Freiherr von Baring', p. 60 and Wissel, *Ruhmwürdige Thaten*, p. 60.

31. Dehnel, *Erinnerungen deutscher Offiziere*, p. 288.

32. Wissel, *Ruhmwürdige Thaten*, p. 183.

33. Beamish, *Geschichte der Königlich Deutschen Legion*, vol. 2, pp. 382–3 gives thirty men. Ludwig von Ompteda, *Ein hannoversch-englischer Offizier vor hundert Jahren: Chris-*

tian Friedrich Wilhelm Freiherr von Omptedo, Oberst und Brigadier in der Königlich-Deutschen Legion. 26 November 1765 bis 18 Juni 1815 (Leipzig, 1892), p. 282, gives 100 men. There is some confusion over the timing of this incident, which Schwertfeger, *Geschichte der Königlich Deutschen Legion*, vol. 1, pp. 615–16, believes to have taken place more than an hour later, but Brandis – who was an eye witness – quite clearly states that it took place just after d'Erlon's first attack. Likewise the report of the Hanoverian General Staff cited in Schwertfeger, *Geschichte der Königlich Deutschen Legion*, vol. 2, pp. 354–5.

34. Thus the assessment of Georg Baring in his 'Geschichthiche Darstellung der Verteidigung von La Haye Sainte am 18 Juni 1815', HStAH Hann 381D, 237, vol. 426.

35. Thus Jens Mastnak and Michael-Andreas Tänzer, *'Diese denckwürdige und mörderische Schlacht': Die Hannoveraner bei Waterloo* (Celle, 2003).

36. Wissel, *Ruhmwürdige Thaten*, p. 130.

37. Hann38D, 243, fol. 47.

38. For these intrepid Lüneburgers see B. von Linsingen, *Aus Hannovers militärischer Vergangenheit* (Hanover, 1880), p. 313.

39. Biedermann, *Erinnerungen*, vol. 1, p. 191.

40. Jacobi, *Erinnerungen*. Quoted in Glover (ed.), *German Sources*, p. 135.

41. Georg Baring, 'Erzählung der Theilnahme des 2. Leichten Bataillons der Königlichen Deutschen Legion an der Schlacht von Waterloo', *Hannoversches Militärisches Journal* (2nd issue, Hanover, 1831), 69–90, 74–5.

42. Wissel, *Ruhmwürdige Thaten*, pp. 130–31.

43. Barbero, *The Battle*, p. 210.

44. Quoted in Cotton, *A Voice from Waterloo*, p. 63.

45. Quoted in Antony Brett-James (ed.), *Napoleon's Last Campaign from Eyewitness Accounts* (London, 1964), p. 145.

46. Quoted in Jane Vansittart (ed.), *Surgeon James's Journals 1815* (London, 1865), pp. 35–6.
47. Biedermann, *Erinnerungen*, vol. 1, p. 192.

5. INFERNO

1. Quoted in Andrew W. Field, *Waterloo. The French Perspective* (Barnsley, 2012), p. 89.
2. Thus Jac Weller, *Wellington at Waterloo* (London, 1967), p. 117. Jean Charras, *Histoire de la campagne de 1815, Waterloo* (Brussels, 1857), pp. 280–82, claims that neither Napoleon nor Ney thought of shelling the farm, which seems unlikely. The damage done to Hougoumont was largely by uncontrolled fires (David Buttery, *Waterloo. Battlefield Guide* (Barnsley, 2013), p. 59), while those at La Haye Sainte were put out in time.
3. Quoted in Field, *Waterloo. The French Perspective*, p. 156.
4. Quoted in Peter Hofschröer, *1815. The Waterloo Campaign. The German Victory* (London, 1999), p. 96.
5. Thus Jonathan Leach, *Rough Sketches of the Life of an Old Soldier* (London, 1831), p. 389, who observed them from his position to the east of the farm.
6. Quoted in Field, *Waterloo. The French Perspective*, pp. 131–2.
7. See Ludwig von Wissel, *Ruhmwürdige Thaten, welche in den letzten Kriegen von Unteroffizieren und Soldaten der englisch-deutschen Legion und der hannoverschen Armee verrichtet sind. Aus zuverlässigen Nachrichten zsgest. von Ludwig von Wissel* (Hanover, 1846), p. 131.
8. Ibid., p. 132.
9. Ibid., pp. 132–3.
10. Ibid., p. 131.
11. Georg Baring, 'Erzählung der Theilnahme des 2. Leichten Bataillons der Königlichen Deutschen Legion an der Schlacht von Waterloo,' *Hannoversches Militärisches Journal* (2nd issue, Hanover, 1831), p. 76.

12. Quoted in Edward Cotton, *A Voice from Waterloo* (London, 1974, first published 1849), p. 88.

13. Edmund Wheatley, *The Wheatley Diary. A Journal and Sketchbook from the Peninsular War and the Waterloo Campaign*, edited with an introduction and notes by Christopher Hibbert (London, 1964), p. 66.

14. N. Ludlow Beamish, *Geschichte der Königlich Deutschen Legion* (2 vols., Berlin, 1906), vol. 2, p. 387.

15. Ibid.

16. Wheatley, *Diary*, p. 66. Wheatley is referring to mortar or howitzer rounds, then battlefield not siege artillery.

17. As described by Rittmeister Wilhelm von Schnehen to Major Bremer, 11.11.1824, HStAH, Hann 41, 152, fols. 9–10.

18. Baring, 'Erzählung der Theilnahme des 2. Leichten Bataillons', p. 76.

19. Ibid., p. 77.

20. Wissel, *Ruhmwürdige Thaten*, p. 183. (The timing of this incident is unclear.)

21. Friedrich Lindau, *A Waterloo Hero. The Reminiscences of Friedrich Lindau*, edited and presented by James Bogle and Andrew Uffindell (London, 2009), p. 169.

22. Ibid., p. 170.

23. Ibid., pp. 170–71.

24. Wissel, *Ruhmwürdige Thaten*, p. 183.

25. Ibid., p. 133.

26. Baring, 'Erzählung der Theilnahme des 2. Leichten Bataillons', p. 77.

27. Thus the account of the head of the allied Field Train Department, Sir Richard D. Henegan, *Seven Years Campaigning in the Peninsula and the Netherlands from 1808 to 1815* (2 vols., London, 1846), vol. 2, pp. 321–2.

28. Cotton, *A Voice from Waterloo*, p. 89.

29. N. Ludlow Beamish, *History of the King's German Legion* (2 vols. London, 1832–7), vol. 2, p. 513.

30. Ludwig von Ompteda, *Ein hannoversch-englischer Offizier vor hundert Jahren. Christian Friedrich Wilhelm Freiherr von Ompteda, Oberst and Brigadier in der Königlich Deutschen Legion. 26 November 1765 bis 18 Juni 1815* (Leipzig, 1892), p. 285.

31. Wheatley, *Diary*, p. 66.

32. Ompteda, *Ein hannoversch-englischer Offizier*, p. 284.

33. Ibid. pp. 282–3; Wissel, *Ruhmwürdige Thaten*, p. 186.

34. Beamish, *Geschichte der Königlich Deutschen Legion*, vol. 2, p. 390.

35. Ompteda, *Ein hannoversch-englischer Offizier*, pp. 283–4. I am assuming that the last attack was the closest shave.

36. See ibid, p. 285.

37. Ibid.

38. For the figures see Mark Adkin, *The Waterloo Companion* (London, 2001), p. 370 and Heinrich Dehnel, *Erinnerungen deutscher Offiziere, in britischen Diensten aus den Kriegsjahren 1805 bis 1816* (Hanover, 1864), p. 285.

39. Ompteda, *Ein hannoversch-englischer Offizier*, p. 285.

40. 'Auszug aus dem Tagebuch des Herzöglich Nassauischen 1. Leichten Infanterie-Regiment im Jahr 1815. Bericht aus dem Tagebuch des Nassauischen 1. Regiments über die Ereignisse vom 15. bis zum 18 Juni', in Julius Pflugk-Harttung, *Belle-Alliance* (Berlin, 1915), p. 198.

41. Thus Baring, 'Erzählung der Theilnahme des 2. Leichten Bataillons', p. 78. The timing is disputed by Bernhard Schwertfeger, *Geschichte der Königlich Deutschen Legion 1803–1816* (2 vols., Hanover, 1907), vol. 1, p. 617.

42. Baring, 'Erzählung der Theilnahme des 2. Leichten Bataillons', p. 79.

43. Lindau, *A Waterloo Hero*, pp. 171–2.

44. Wissel, *Ruhmwürdige Thaten*, p. 131.

45. Baring, 'Erzählung der Theilnahme des 2. Leichten Bataillons', p. 80.

46. Wissel, *Ruhmwürdige Thaten*, pp. 158–9, 155.

47. Lindau, *A Waterloo Hero*, p. 170.
48. Baring, 'Erzählung der Theilnahme des 2. Leichten Bataillons', pp. 80–81.
49. Beamish, *Geschichte der Königlich Deutschen Legion*, vol. 2, p. 395.
50. Baring, 'Erzählung der Theilnahme des 2. Leichten Bataillons', p. 81.
51. Ibid., p. 82.

6. HAND TO HAND

1. Edmund Wheatley, *The Wheatley Diary. A Journal and Sketchbook from the Peninsular War and the Waterloo Campaign*, edited with an introduction and notes by Christopher Hibbert (London, 1964), p. 68.
2. N. Ludlow Beamish, *Geschichte der Königlich Deutschen Legion* (2 vols., Berlin, 1906), vol. 2, p. 396.
3. Georg Baring, 'Erzählung der Theilnahme des 2. Leichten Bataillons der Königlichen Deutschen Legion an der Schlacht von Waterloo', *Hannoversches Militärisches Journal* (2nd issue, Hanover, 1831), p. 82.
4. Friedrich Lindau, *A Waterloo Hero. The Reminiscences of Friedrich Lindau*, edited and presented by James Bogle and Andrew Uffindell (London, 2009), pp. 172–3.
5. Bernhard Schwertfeger, *Geschichte der Königlich Deutschen Legion 1803–1816* (2 vols., Hanover, 1907), vol. 1, p. 618.
6. Lindau, *A Waterloo Hero*, p. 172.
7. Baring, 'Erzählung der Theilnahme des 2. Leichten Bataillons', p. 83.
8. Ludwig von Wissel, *Ruhmwürdige Thaten, welche in den letzten Kriegen von Unteroffizieren und Soldaten der englisch-deutschen Legion und der hannoverschen Armee verrichtet sind. Aus zuverlässigen Nachrichten zsgest. von Ludwig von Wissel* (Hanover, 1846), p. 183.

9. On Mevius, Lindhorst and Lindenau see ibid., p. 131.

10. Lindau describes Graeme saving Frank (*A Waterloo Hero*, p. 173). Graeme's account of being saved is in Antony Brett-James (ed.), *Napoleon's Last Campaign from Eyewitness Accounts* (London, 1964). I am assuming that the two incidents were separate and not somehow conflated or misremembered by the witnesses, which is possible.

11. Wissel, *Ruhmwürdige Thaten*, p. 135.

12. Julius von Pflugk-Harttung, *Vorgeschichte der Schlacht bei Belle-Alliance. Wellington* (Berlin, 1903), p. 198.

13. Schwertfeger, *Geschichte der Königlich Deutschen Legion*, vol. 1, p. 619.

14. Lindau, *A Waterloo Hero*, p. 173.

15. Wissel, *Ruhmwürdige Thaten*, p. 132.

16. Baring, 'Erzählung der Theilnahme des 2. Leichten Bataillons', p. 84.

17. Brett-James (ed.), *Napoleon's Last Campaign*, p. 146.

18. John Kincaid, *Adventures in the Rifle Brigade and Random Shots from a Rifleman (abridged) by Captain Sir John Kincaid* (London, 1981), p. 168. For the other side, see Andrew W. Field, *Waterloo. The French Perspective* (Barnsley, 2012), pp. 170–75.

19. Jonathan Leach, *Rough Sketches of the Life of an Old Soldier* (London, 1831), p. 390.

20. Edward Cotton, *A Voice from Waterloo* (London, 1974; first published 1849), pp. 97–9.

21. Schwertfeger, *Geschichte der Königlich Deutschen Legion*, vol. 1, p. 621, suggests south, whereas the eyewitness description by Lieutenant Pontéecourlant (which I take to refer to the same battery) suggests west of the farm: see Field, *Waterloo. The French Perspective*, p. 173.

22. Quoted in Alessandro Barbero, *The Battle. A New History of Waterloo* (London, 2005), p. 320.

23. See the account by the topographical engineer W. R. Craan, *An Historical Account of the Battle of Waterloo Intended to*

Explain and Elucidate the Topographical Plan (Brussels, 1817), pp. 21 and 28.

24. Kincaid, *Adventures in the Rifle Brigade*, p. 170. See also Leach, *Rough Sketches*, p. 391.

25. Quoted in Field, *Waterloo. The French Perspective*, p. 175.

26. Baring, 'Erzählung der Theilnahme des 2. Leichten Bataillons', p. 84.

27. Ludwig von Ompteda, *Ein hannoversch-englischer Offizier vor hundert Jahren: Christian Friedrich Wilhelm Freiherr von Ompteda, Oberst and Brigadier in der Königlich Deutschen Legion. 26 November 1765 bis 18 Juni 1815* (Leipzig, 1892), p. 286.

28. Heinrich Dehnel, *Erinnerungen deutscher Offiziere in britischen Diensten aus den Kriegsjahren 1805 bis 1816* (Hanover, 1864), p. 290.

29. Lindau, *A Waterloo Hero*, p. 174.

30. See Barbero, *The Battle*, p. 315.

31. For a description of the terrain see Dehnel, *Erinnerungen deutscher Offiziere*, p. 288.

32. Wheatley, *Diary*, p. 70.

33. See Ompteda, *Ein hannoversch-englischer Offizier*, p. 287.

34. The description of Captain Berger is in ibid., p. 288.

35. Wheatley, *Diary*, p. 71.

36. Cotton, *A Voice from Waterloo*, p. 89.

37. Baring, 'Erzählung der Theilnahme des 2. Leichten Bataillons', p. 86.

38. Quoted in Barbero, *The Battle*, p. 345.

39. Dehnel, *Erinnerungen deutscher Offiziere*, p. 291.

40. Baring, 'Erzählung der Theilnahme des 2. Leichten Bataillons', p. 87.

41. Quoted in Dehnel, *Erinnerungen deutscher Offiziere*, p. 291.

42. See the account in Georg Baring's fullest report: 'Geschichtliche Darstellung der Verteidigung von La Haye Sainte am 18 Juni 1815', HStAH, Hann38D, 237, fols. 437–8.

43. Bericht des nassauischen 1. Regiments über die Ereignisse vom 15. bis zum 18. Juni', in Julius von Pflugk-Harttung, *Belle-Alliance (Verbündetes Heer). Berichte und Angaben über die Beteiligung deutscher Truppen der Armee Wellingtons an dem Gefechte bei Quatrebras und der Schlacht bei Belle-Alliance* (Berlin, 1915), p. 199.

44. Wheatley, *Diary*, p. 72.

45. Leach, *Rough Sketches*. p. 394, describing the day after the battle, almost certainly from his vantage point close to the farm.

46. The casualty figures are in Lt B. Riefkugel, 'Effectiver Bestand des vormaligen 2ten Leichten Bataillons der K. D. Legion in der Schlacht von Waterloo', HStAH, Hann41, 152, fol. 45.

47. I have used some dramatic licence here, based on the account in Baring, 'Erzählung der Theilnahme des 2. Leichten Bataillons', pp. 89–90.

48. Thus the text by Georg Baumann, 'Killed in the battle of Waterloo. Names on King's German Legion at the Waterloo Column at Hanover'. I thank Mr Baumann for letting me have sight of this document.

49. For Kincaid's similar experience, see Barbero, *The Battle*, p. 411.

50. Wheatley, *Diary*, p. 74.

51. Emanuel Biedermann, *Erinnerungen, Wanderungen, Erfahrungen und Lebensansichten eines froh- und freisinnigen Schweizers* (2 vols., Trogen, 1828), vol. 1, pp. 193–4.

7. 'HEAT AND CENTRE OF THE STRIFE'

1. Alessandro Barbero, *The Battle. A New History of Waterloo* (London, 2005), p. 423.

2. In addition to other examples of the centrality of La Haye Sainte see the report of the Nassauers in Julius Pflugk-Harttung, *Belle Alliance* (Berlin, 1915), p. 205.

3. Thus Ian Fletcher, *A Desperate Business. Wellington, the British Army and the Waterloo Campaign* (Staplehurst, 2001), p. 116.

4. Thus Edmund Wheatley, *The Wheatley Diary. A Journal and Sketchbook from the Peninsular War and the Waterloo Campaign*, edited with an introduction and notes by Christopher Hibbert (London, 1964), p. 67.

5. Ompteda's brigade had the greatest KGL casualties: Daniel S. Gray, 'The services of the King's German Legion in the army of the Duke of Wellington, 1809–1815' (DPhil dissertation, Florida State University, 1970), p. 336.

6. See John Keegan, *The Face of Battle* (London and New York, 1976), pp. 164–8.

7. For casualties see Otto Puffahrt (ed.), *In der Schlacht von Waterloo gefallene, verwundete und vermisste Soldaten aus der Hannoverschen Armee* (Lüneburg, 2004), pp. 70–77.

8. For a recent overview see Edward Madigan, 'Courage and cowardice in wartime', *War in History*, 20 (2013), 4–6.

9. For the original concept as applied to military sociology see Edward A. Shils and Morris Janowitz, 'Cohesion and disintegration in the Wehrmacht in World War II', *Public Opinion Quarterly*, Summer 1948, 280–315, especially 283–8. There is a recent discussion of this immense debate in Guy L. Siebold, 'The essence of military group cohesion', *Armed Forces and Society*, 33 (2007), 286–94.

10. For a vivid description of this phenomenon in the Second World War see Robert Sterling Rush, *Hell in Huertgen Forest. The Ordeal and Triumph of an American Infantry Regiment* (Lawrence, KS, 2001).

11. On the importance of ideological motivations see Omer Bartov, *The Eastern Front, 1941–1945. German Troops and the Barbarisation of Warfare* (2nd edn, New York, 2001).

12. See Kurt Ihlefeld (ed.), *Preussischer Choral. Deutscher Soldatenglaube in drei Jahrhunderten* (Berlin, 1935), pp. 81, 113 re Napoleonic Wars. There is nothing on the Hanoverians.

13. I owe this insight to Ilya Berkovich. For some interesting reflections on 'honour' and the defence of La Haye Sainte see also Mastnak and Tänzer, '*Diese denckwürdige und mörderische Schlacht*', p. 52.

14. Michael Broers, '"Civilized, rational behaviour"? The concept of surrender in the Revolutionary and Napoleonic Wars, 1792–1815', in Hew Strachan and Holger Afflerbach (eds.), *How Fighting Ends. A History of Surrender* (Oxford, 2012), pp. 229–38 (especially p. 232).

8. LEGACY: A 'GERMAN VICTORY'?

1. See the printed General Orders of the Field Marshal Duke of Cambridge, Headquarters, Hanover, StAH, Hann38D, 237, fol. 111.

2. Manfred Bresemann, 'The King's German Legion 1803–1816 and the British Traditions Handed down by the Legion to the Royal Hanoverian Army up to 1866' (typescript, NAM-355-453-3), p. 14.

3. Quoted in Bernhard Schwertfeger, *Peninsula-Waterloo. Zum Gedächtnis der Königlich Deutschen Legion*, printed version of lecture held in February 1914, p. 27.

4. I am heavily indebted here to Jasper Heinzen, 'Transnational affinities and invented traditions: the Napoleonic wars in British and Hanoverian memory, 1815–1915', *English Historical Review*, 97, 529 (2012), 1404–34.

5. Doctor Wilhelm Blumenhagen, *Waterloo. Eine vaterländische Ode* (Hanover, 1816).

6. *Hannoversches Magazin*, 19.4.1816. For the situation in Prussia see Christopher Clark, 'The wars of liberation in Prussian memory: reflections on the memorialisation of war in early nineteenth-century Germany', *Journal of Modern History*, 68 (1996), 550–76.

7. *Hannoversches Magazin*, 6.1.1830.

8. See Marianne Zehnpfennig, 'Waterloomonument und Bauten am Waterlooplatz', in Harold Hammer-Schenk and Günther Kokkelink (eds.), *Laves und Hannover. Niedersächsische Architektur im neunzehnten Jahrhundert* (Hanover, 1989), pp. 295–302, and more generally, Gerhard Schneider, *'Nicht umsonst gefallen?': Kriegerdenkmäler und Kriegstotenkult in Hannover* (Hannoversche Geschichtsblätter, Sonderband, Hanover, 1991), pp. 31–47.

9. Following the description by Stella Child in Bexhill Hanoverian Study Group, *Newsletter* 43 (April 2005), p. 1.

10. See 'Berechnung über Einnahme und Ausgabe des King's German Legion Unterstützungsfonds, I Januar bis 31 Dezember 1863', printed Hanover 5.2.1864, in HStAH, Hann91, Cordemann, fols. 211–14.

11. As recorded in 'List of officers of the King's German Legion who have died since the disbandment of that corps on the 24 February 1816', HStAH, Hann38D, 243, fols. 23–4.

12. Details for this paragraph and the following one are taken from three typescripts in the National Army Museum by Terry Cooper which update and consolidate the information available elsewhere: 'The King's German Legion Waterloo Roll Call' (York, 1992) NAM 93–27; 'The King's German Legion Waterloo Roll of Officers' (York, 1998) NAM 1998-10-268-1; and 'Officers of the King's German Legion, 1803–1806' (York, 1999) NAM 1999-03-138-1-1.

13. Thus Heise to Benne, 3.11.1841 [no place given], Gareth Glover (ed.), *Letters from the Battle of Waterloo: Unpublished Correspondence by Allied Officers from the Siborne Papers* (London, 2004), p. 234.

14. This paragraph is based on Bresemann, 'The King's German Legion, 1803–1816', pp. 1, 19, 24 *et passim*. See also Joachim Niemeyer, *Königlich Hannoversches Militär 1815–1866* (Beckum, 1992), p. 5.

15. For an introduction to the subject of historical memory in Germany see Alon Confino, 'Telling about Germany: narra-

tives of memory and culture', *Journal of Modern History*, 76 (2004).

16. My thinking on this has been heavily influenced by Jasper Heinzen, 'Hohenzollern state-building in the province of Hanover, 1866–1914' (unpublished PhD dissertation, University of Cambridge, 2010), especially pp. 116–28. He has also supplied me with all the newspaper references for the 1915 anniversary commemorations.

17. See John C. G. Röhl, 'Der Kaiser und England', in Wilfried Rogsch (ed.), *Vicky and Albert, Vicky & the Kaiser* (Ostfildern-Ruit, 1997), pp. 165–86.

18. Schwertfeger, *Peninsula-Waterloo,* p. 3.

19. See Georg Baring, 'Geschichtliche Darstellung der Verteidigung von La Haye Sainte am 18 Juni 1815', HStAH, Hann38D, 237, fols. 423–39.

20. See Gerhard Schneider, 'Die Waterloo gedenkefeier 1915', *Hannoversche Geschichtsblätter*, 65 (2011), 233.

21. See also Wilhelm Pessler, 'Deutsche Waterloo-Erinnerungen im Vaterländischen Museum der Stadt Hanover', *Hannoversche Geschichtsblätter*, 18 (1915), 293–338; idem, 'Die Waterloo-Jahrhundert-Austellung im Vaterländischen Museum der Stadt Hannover', *Hannoversche Geschichtsblätter*, 18 (1915), 389–416.

22. The 'sworn enemies' part of the quote comes from 'Die Waterloo-Ausstellung des Vaterländischen Museum', *Hannoverscher Kurier*, 17.6.1915, no. 31834, evening edition, p. 5. The Suetonius paraphrase in the second half of the quotation is in 'Besuch von Waterloo', *Hannoverscher Kurier*, 18.6.1915, no. 31836, evening edition, p. 5.

23. See Jasper Heinzen, 'A negotiated truce: the battle for Waterloo in European memory since the second world war', *History and Memory*, 26, 1 (Spring/Summer 2014), 39–74.

24. See Andrew W. Field, *Waterloo. The French Perspective* (Barnsley, 2012), p. 3.

25. Jean Charras, *Histoire de la campagne de 1815, Waterloo* (Brussels, 1857), p. 279.

26. For some modelling by a team of professional surveyors and archaeologists of how the original battlefield probably looked see Daniel Schnurr, James Kavanagh and Paul Hill, 'Wellington était-il géométre? RTK GPS révéle Waterloo' (2003), especially pp. 5–11. Accessed under http://www.fig.net/pub/fig_2003/ts_19/pp19_3_schnurr_et_al.pdf (despite the title, the text is in English).

27. The change was already noted by Victor Hugo, *Les Misárables,* translated and with an introduction by Norman Denny (1st edn, 1862; Penguin Classics, one-volume edn, 1982), p. 297. For the perspective of an informed modern battlefield guide see David Buttery, *Waterloo. Battlefield Guide* (Barnsley, 2013), pp. 3–4 and 63–4.

28. *Waterloo. Histoire d'une bataille,* a film written and directed by Jerome Waquet.

29. On this see Peter Hofschröer, *Wellington's Smallest Victory. The Duke, the Model Maker and the Secret of Waterloo* (London, 2004).

30. E.g. Manfred Schlenke, *England und das friderizianische Preussen, 1740–1763. Ein Beitrag zum Verhältnis von Politik und öffentlicher Meinung im England des 18. Jahrhunderts* (Freiburg and Munich, 1963).

31. General Orders, Headquarters, Hanover, 1.2.1816, HStAH, Hann38D, 237, fol. 111.

32. John Kincaid, *Adventures in the Rifle Brigade and Random Shots from a Rifleman (abridged) by Captain Sir John Kincaid* (London, 1981), pp. 171–2.

33. Jonathan Leach, *Rough Sketches of the Life of an Old Soldier* (London, 1831), p. 390.

34. Julius von Pflugk-Harttung, *Vorgeschichte der Schlacht bei Belle-Alliance. Wellington* (Berlin, 1903), p. 1.

35. Quoted in Charles Moore, 'Still skirmishing over the battle of Waterloo', *Daily Telegraph,* 15.9.2013.

36. Julius Runnebaum, *General Karl von Alten: Ein Soldat Europas* (Hildesheim, 1964).
37. See the printed General Orders of the Field Marshal Duke of Cambridge, Headquarters, Hanover, HStAH, Hann38D, 237, fol. 111.

APPENDICES

1. Jac Weller, *Wellington at Waterloo* (London, 1967).
2. John Keegan, *The Face of Battle* (London and New York, 1976), pp. 117–203.
3. Alessandro Barbero, *The Battle. A New History of Waterloo* (London, 2003); Mark Adkin, *The Waterloo Companion* (London, 2001).
4. Torsten Riotte, *Hannover in der britischen Politik (1792–1815). Dynastische Verbindung als Element aussenpolitischer Entscheidungsprozesse* (Münster, 2005); Christopher D. Thompson, 'The Hanoverian dimension in early nineteenth-century British politics', in Brendan Simms and Torsten Riotte (eds.), *The Hanoverian Dimension in British History, 1714–1837* (Cambridge, 2007), pp. 86–110. Peter Hofschröer, *The Hanoverian Army of the Napoleonic Wars* (London, 1989); *1815. The Waterloo Campaign. The German Victory* (London, 1999); *1815. The Waterloo Campaign: Wellington, his German Allies and the Battles of Ligny and Quatre Bras* (London, 1998); Mark Wishon, *German Forces and the British Army. Interactions and Perceptions, 1742–1815* (Basingstoke, 2013). See also the source collection of Klaus-Jürgen Bremm, *Die Königlich Deutsche Legion, 1803–1816 Dokumente zur Militärgeschichte, Deutsches Militärarchiv* (no date or place of publication).
5. There is a vivid description in Andrew Uffindell and Michael Corum, *On the Fields of Glory. The Battlefields of the 1815 Campaign* (London and Stackpoole, PA, 1996), pp. 117–31.

6. Barbero, *Waterloo*, pp. 149–56, 238–43 and 307–15.

7. Hofschröer, *1815. The Waterloo Campaign*, pp. 89–92, 104–5, 131–5. Daniel S. Gray, 'The services of the King's German Legion in the army of the Duke of Wellington, 1809–1815' (PhD dissertation, Florida State University, 1969), 337–50, provides valuable background but does not add much on the battle itself.

8. See Martin Mittelacher, 'Die Nassauer bei Waterloo', *Nassauische Annalen*, 109 (1998), 265–75; idem, 'Die Nassauer bei Waterloo. Aus der Sicht neuerer englisch-sprachiger Literatur', *Nassauische Annalen*, 109 (1998), 265–75; Jochem Rudersdorf, 'Prinz Wilhelm von Oranien, Wellington und die Nassauer bei Quatre-Bras und Waterloo', *Nassauische Annalen*, 120 (2009), 279–320.

9. Jens Mastnak and Michael-Andreas Tänzer, '*Diese denkwürdige und mörderische Schlacht'. Die Hannoveraner bei Waterloo* (Celle, 2003), pp. 5–7.

10. Bernard Coppens and Patrice Courcelle, *La Haie-Sainte. Waterloo 1815*, Les Carnets de la Campagne 3 (2000).

11. Wilhelm von Schnehen to Major Bremer, Gross Schmeen, 11.11.1824, HStAH, Hann41, 152, fol. 7.

12. Heise to Benne, Hanover, 24.1.1841, in Gareth Glover (ed.), *Letters from the Battle of Waterloo: Unpublished Correspondence by Allied Officers from the Siborne Papers* (London, 2004), p. 233.

13. Glover (ed.), *Letters from the Battle of Waterloo*.

14. Julius von Pflugk-Harttung, *Belle-Alliance (Verbündetes Heer). Berichte und Angaben über die Beteiligung deutscher Truppen der Armee Wellingtons an dem Gefechte bei Quatrebras und der Schlacht bei Belle-Alliance* (Berlin, 1915), pp. 106–11, 117, 120–26, 195–200, 257–8.

15. Gareth Glover (ed.), *The Waterloo Archive. Volume II: German Sources* (Barnsley, 2010). His fifth volume, which includes very useful translations of some of the previously unused German-language sources, appeared after the first

draft of this book was complete: Gareth Glover (ed.), *The Waterloo Archive. Volume V. German Sources* (London, 2013).

16. Andrew W. Field, *Waterloo. The French Perspective* (Barnsley, 2012), pp. 51, 57, 89–96, 170–75.

17. Georg Baring, 'Erzählung der Theilnahme des 2. Leichten Bataillons der Königlichen Deutschen Legion an der Schlacht von Waterloo', *Hannoversches Militarisches Journal* (2nd issue, Hanover, 1831), 69–90; Georg Baring, 'Geschichtliche Darstellung der Verteidigung von La Haye Sainte am 18 Juni 1815', HStAH, Hann38D, 237, fols. 423–39.

18. HStAH, Hann38D, 243.

19. Friedrich Lindau, *A Waterloo Hero. The Reminiscences of Friedrich Lindau*, edited and presented by James Bogle and Andrew Uffindell (London, 2009).

20. Ludwig von Wissel, *Ruhmwürdige Thaten, welche in den letzten Kriegen von Unteroffizieren und Soldaten der englisch-deutschen Legion und der Hannoverschen Armee verrichtet sind. Aus zuverlässigen Nachrichten zsgest. von Ludwig von Wissel* (Hanover, 1846). See also 'Auszüge aus den Papieren des König Guelphen Ordens [*sic*] ausgezeichnete Thaten von Unteroffizieren und Mannschaften der K. G. Legion, betreffend 1803 bis 1816', HStAH, Hann38D, 239, fol. 4 (re the role of the officers). D. D. Vigors, 'Voices from the Napoleonic Wars', minutes of the Proceedings of the Royal Artillery Institution (no date), 137–140 focuses almost exclusively on the KGL artillery.

21. See the reflections in Mastnak and Tänzer, *Diese Denkwürdige*, p. 6, Leighton S. James, *Witnessing the Revolutionary and Napoleonic Wars in German Central Europe* (Basingstoke, 2013), pp. 5–6 and (more generally) in Michael Epkenhans, Stig Förster and Karen Hagemann (eds.), *Militärische Erinnerungskultur. Soldaten im Spiegel von Biographien, Memoiren, und Selbstzeugnissen* (Paderborn, 2006).

Index

(the full name is given if known, otherwise the rank and second name)

Abba pop group, xv, 129
Adkin, Mark, 130
Albert (Lieutenant), 45
Alexander, Tsar, xvi
Alix's 1st Division (French), 7, 102
Almutz, Frederick, 13
Ammunition, 28, 67–68, 69, 72, 74–75, 76, 77–78, 80, 82, 83, 94, 109, 112
Amputations, 53, 110, 115
Artillery, 37, 38, 45, 56, 60, 62, 67, 69, 72, 75, 89, 101, 118, 161(n16)
  Allied, 2, 10, 12, 23, 35, 87
  French cannon balls sticking in mud, 34
  horse artillery, 83
Aulard's brigade (French), 43, 50, 53, 102

Baker rifles, 11
  loading process for muskets/ rifles, 40–41, 66
  musket vs. rifle firing rate/ accuracy, 40
  problems with, 41–42
Baltic area, 11
Barbero, Alessandro, 129
Baring, Ensign Louis, 96
Baring, Major George, 23, 35, 39, 43, 48, 49, 52, 65
  achievement of, 126–127
  and ammunition shortage, 75, 76, 78, 79, 112, 114
  comrades shouting to shoot him, 95
  and courage and ferocity of enemy, 58
  and courage of his men, 67
  on day after battle, 98
  death of, 114, 117
  early life of, 19–20
  ennobled in Britain and Hanover, 112

Baring, Major George,
  (*continued*)
  forces under, 26–28, 54, 54,
    82, 94, 96, 149(n1),
    155(n14)
  and Friedrich Lindau, 74
  on horseback, 60, 75, 85, 94
  ignored by officers and men,
    94, 97
  joins 1st Hussar Regiment, 96
  ordering retreat, 79–80
  overseeing roll-call after
    battle, 96–97
  reports of, 114–115, 120, 134
  in Spain, 20
  speech at Garrison Church of
    Hanover, 111–112
Barricade across Brussels road,
  25, 35, 43, 50, 52, 56, 58
Battle, The (Barbero), 129
Bavaria, 10
Beamish, Colonel North Ludlow,
  113, 134
Belgian civilians, 3
Beneke, Christoph, 59
Berger (Captain), 90
Bexhill base camp, 11, 13, 34, 97,
  108
  Bexhill as Bexhill-on-Sea, 14
Biedermann, Lieutenant Emanuel,
  2, 6, 16, 24, 43, 49, 54,
  106, 134
  death of, 116
  at night before battle, 8
  pitying Belgian civilians, 3
  united with battalion, 98
Black, Jeremy, xv
Blücher, Marshal, 1, 58, 69, 95

Blumenhagen, Dr Wilhelm, 112
Bonaparte, Napoleon, 9, 55–57,
  121, 131, 160(n2)
  and attack at crossroads,
    92–93
  as close to beating Wellington
    twice, 101
  determined to take
    farmhouse, 68–69
  exile in Elba, xvi, 11
  hoping to frighten Allied
    forces, 38–39
  mistakes made by, 102–103
  and Ney's request for troops,
    83
  at night and morning before
    battle, 29–30
  number of men at disposal of,
    30
  planning for battle, 31
Bondarchuk, Sergei, 131
Bonnet (commander of 51st
  Ligne), 53
Bösewiel (acting-Major), 26, 43, 54
Bourgeois's 2nd Brigade in Alix's
  1st Division (French), 7,
  102
Bramall, Field-Marshal Edwin
  Lord, 126
Brandis (*aide de camp*), 86, 91,
  93, 94, 159(n33)
Breithaupt, Friedrich, 80
Bremen Field Battalion, 6
British 5th Regiment/Division, 2,
  44
British Household and Union
  Cavalry Brigades, 50, 51,
  103

British War Office, 10
Brooks, Eliza, 117
Brunswick Hussars, 2, 126
Brussels, hospital in, 98
Bühren, Corporal W., 48
Burt, Mary Anne, 14
Bush (Busch), Henry, 14, 97
Bylandt's Dutch-Belgian brigade, 22, 34
Byron, George Gordon, xvi

Cambridge, Duke of, 123, 126
Canler (Corporal), 7, 28–29, 37, 52
Carey (Lieutenant), 49, 73, 82
Carl (Lieutenant), 96
Casualties
    Allied, 12, 34, 35, 43, 44, 46–47, 54, 59, 61, 72, 80, 81, 82, 84, 85, 86, 90, 95–96, 96–97, 98, 104, 105, 167(n5)
    deaths after battle, 98
    French, 37, 39–40, 44, 52–54, 60, 66, 69, 70, 79, 86, 95–96, 102
Cathcart (Lord), 25
Cavalry, 28, 36, 37, 42, 46, 48, 50, 60, 61–62, 63, 70, 71, 83, 84, 86, 87, 113
    British, 46, 50, 51, 52, 88, 93, 103
    as danger to infantry, 47
    riderless/wounded mounts, 69, 93
    See also Cuirassiers
Charras, Jean, 121
Charrier, Baptist, 10

Childe Harold (Byron), xvi
Churchill, Winston, xvii
Clover leaf emblem, 18
Cobbett, William, 13
Cohesion in combat, 105–109
Coppens, Bernard, 131
Cornwell, Bernard, 124
Corporal punishment, 107
Cotton, Edward, 67
Courage in combat, 105–106, 110
Courcelle, Patrice, 131
Crabbée (Colonel), 48
Crosse (eagle-bearer), 17
Cuirassiers, 37, 46, 48, 49, 51, 56, 63, 83, 89, 91–92, 95, 99, 105
    individual encounter with injured hussar, 92
    See also Cavalry

Dahrendorf, Ludwig, 59, 68, 82, 115
    carrying on after wounds, 104
de Lancey (Quartermaster), 21
Demobilization of forces after battle, 115
Denmark, 10
d'Erlon's 1st Corps (French), 7, 31, 36, 50, 51, 55, 57, 62, 77, 93, 101, 102
    Durutte's division, 52, 57
Desales (artillery commander), 29, 34
Desertions, 106–107
Devienne (Colonel), 102
Diaries, 12

Dobritzky, Alexander, 10
Donzelot 2nd Infantry Division
  (French), 37, 102
Dragoons, 25, 63
Drill regulations, 118
Duels, 20

Ebeling, Henry, 13
Engineers, 22, 23, 24, 30, 43, 58,
  109
Eugene of Savoy, 123

Fabian, Corporal Ludwig, 74
Federal Republic of Germany, 121
Ferdinand, Prince Karl Wilhelm
  of Brunswick, 123
Fichermont wood, 57
Field, Andrew, 134
Field kettles, 72–73
1st Battalion of 51st Ligne
  (French), 102
1st Hussar Regiment, 96, 113
1st Light Battalion King's
  German Legion, 6, 14, 22,
  23, 27, 45, 48, 54, 65, 82,
  91, 106
  in the Peninsula and Southern
    France, 17
  proportion of Hanoverians in,
    10
5th British Infantry Division, 28
Flogging routines, 118
Frank, Ensign George, 49, 80–81,
  91, 164(n10)
  commemorated with plaque
    in home town, 112
  death of, 117
Frederick the Great, 123

French forces, 28–29
  1st and 2nd Corps, 31–32
    (*see also* d'Erlon's 1st
    Corps; Reille's 2nd Corps)
  casualties, 102 (*see also*
    Casualties: French)
  first contact with enemy, 37
  fortitude of, 109–110
  at night before battle, 7
  occupation of Hanover in
    1803, 9
  in retreat, 95
  two-column attacks on
    farmhouse, 70–71, 78
  veterans' loyalty to the
    emperor, 6, 7
  See also individual units

Gardner (Major), 124
Genappe, meadow near, 2
Gentry (French commander), 102
George III of England, 9
German Empire, 119
German military tradition, 127
Gerson, Georg Hartog, 17, 26,
  61, 118
Glover, Gareth, 133–134
Göbel, Ensign Christian, 116
Goethe, Johann Wolfgang, 133
Gourgaud (General), 30
Graeme, Lieutenant John
  Drummond, 26, 27, 36, 43,
  49, 50, 51, 52, 53, 59, 65,
  164(n10)
  covering retreat, 79–80,
    80–81, 82–83
  wounded in hand, 85
  in years after battle, 117–118

Greenword, Cox and Company,
11
Grouchy (Marshal), 30, 55, 121
Guards Brigade, 22

Halkett's brigade, 85
Hamburg, 9
Hannover in der britischen Politik
(Riotte), 130
Hannoverscher Kurier, 120
Hannoversches Magazin,
112–113
Hanover, 9, 11
'Guelphic Medal' instituted
by, 134
Hanoverian army, 19, 118,
149(n2)
Hanoverian forces, 10, 13,
61, 84, 94, 105, 108, 112,
119, 126 (*see also*
Lüneburg Light Battalion)
Hanoverian Legion (French
sponsored), 15
Hanoverian State Archives,
xii, xvii, 115
Hanoverian Study Group,
124
invaded by Prussia, 119
Kingdom of Hanover, 111
Personal Union with Great
Britain, 130
Vaterländische Museum in,
120, 122
Waterloo column in, 113, 121
Harz (Rifleman), 24, 25, 40
Haselden, Harriet, 14, 97
Haxo (General), 30, 32
Hegener, Friedrich, 59–60

Heinecke, Friedrich, 16
Heinz, George (Gottfried), 14,
113
Heinzen, Jasper, 170(n16)
Heise (medic), 27, 53, 82
Heise, Captain Christoph, 45–46,
132–133
Heise, Corporal Heinrich, 80, 81
Hennes, John, 13
Hofschröer, Peter, 125, 130
Holland, 10
Holtzermann, Captain Adolph,
82
Holtzermann, Captain Ernest
Augustus, 86, 117
Holtzermann, Captain Philip, 14,
26, 34, 86
Holy Roman Empire, 16, 126
Honour, 19, 75, 76, 80, 94, 98,
108, 109, 124, 127
Hougoumont château, 22, 23, 24,
31, 33, 57, 93, 103, 123,
124
battle compared to La Haye
Sainte battle, 104
damaged by fires, 160(n2)
defence of, 130
Hubart (Adjutant-Major), 36
Hugo, Victor, xv, 122, 127,
171(n27)

Iberian Peninsula, 11, 20
Ideology and combat cohesion,
107–108
Imperial Guard (French), 31, 93,
95, 123, 125
Ireland, 11, 108
Italy, 108, 121

Jacobi, Captain Carl, 33, 49
James, John Haddy, 53

Keegan, John, 104–105, 129
Kempt, Sir James, 87–88
  Kempt's brigade, 85
Kessler (Lieutenant), 96
KGL. *See* King's German Legion
Kielmannsegg's brigade, 84
Kincaid, Captain Johnny, 35, 38,
  83, 84, 124
King's German Legion (KGL)
  accepted in English society, 13
  as agent of cultural transfer
    after battle, 118
  anniversary of founding, 119
  casualties in Ompteda's
    brigade, 167(n5) (*see also*
    Casualties: Allied)
  collective contribution of,
    112–113
  disbanded after battle, 111
  engineering units, 22, 23
  establishment of, 9, 119
  5th Line Battalion, 17, 23, 26,
    45, 46, 61, 62, 69, 70, 71,
    72, 85, 87, 89, 90, 91, 97,
    105, 106, 113, 116, 117
  8th Line Battalion, 22–23, 45,
    46–47, 91, 105, 106, 113,
    116
  fund for widows and orphans
    of ex-Legionnaires, 115
  Germanization of, 119
  Hanoverians executed for
    recruiting for, 10
  legacy of in Britain, 123
  officers after battle, 115–117

  as part of British regular
    army, 11–12
  regarded with ambivalence in
    Germany, 119
  relations between officers and
    men, 14–15
  retreat from farmhouse, 76,
    79–80
  silver centrepiece
    commemorating, 113–114
  as socially diverse, 17
  3rd King's German Legion
    Hussar Regiment, 92
  transferred to Hanoverian
    service in 1816, 123
  See also 1st Light Battalion
    King's German Legion; 2nd
    Light Battalion King's
    German Legion
Kloppe, C., 48

La Haie-Sainte. Waterloo 1815
  (Coppens and Courcelle),
  131
La Haye Sainte, farm of, xvii, 22,
  23–24
  barn door removed at, 25, 42,
    43, 49–50, 59, 78
  barn set on fire, 68, 73, 78
  battle for won by Allies, 96
  breach in main gate at, 79
  as breakwater for French
    advance, 56
  Brussels road near, 25
    (*see also* Barricade across
    Brussels road)
  commemorative plaque on
    wall of farmhouse, 124

compared with fighting at
  Hougoumont, 104
current description of, 122
described, 4–5
as focus of French military
  plan. 31–32, 101–102
French failure to thoroughly
  prepare the capture of, 32
French infantry in, 83
French memorial related to,
  122
Germans herded out of barn,
  87
kitchen garden at, 49, 51, 53,
  54, 65–66, 79, 80, 83, 107
legacy of in Britain, 123–125
loopholes in courtyard walls,
  25, 44, 59, 73, 79, 83
mistakes made by Napoleon
  and Wellington concerning,
  102–103
national origins of men at, 10
occupied by German Legion,
  4
on-site interpretation of,
  122–123
orchard at, 4, 5, 6, 27, 28, 35,
  36, 39, 42, 47–48, 54
origin of name, 4
recapture of farmhouse, 87
regiments in buildings of, 106
sandpit at, 28, 35, 38, 43, 44,
  51, 52, 67, 84
sunken road behind, 5, 34,
  45, 47, 54, 63, 82, 85, 89,
  90, 91, 93, 94, 97
tactical value of farmhouse,
  83

thunderstorm/rain before
  battle at, 2–3, 5
withdrawal from, 79–80. 104
Lancers, 63
Languages, English/German,
  12–13, 113, 125
Leach, Captain Jonathan, 5, 38,
  83, 96, 124, 157(n6),
  166(n45)
Le Caillou, farm at, 29
Le Haye village, 22
Lehmann, Simon, 5
Levavasseur, Octave, 58, 109
Life Guards (French), 51, 53
Ligny, 1
Lindam, Captain Ole, 117
Lindau, Friedrich, 1, 5, 16, 24,
  25, 59, 134, 164(n10)
  carrying on after wounds,
    104
  covering retreat, 80
  gesture of mercy by, 64–65
  taken as prisoner, 81–82, 86,
    87
  taking canteen of wine from
    cellar, 6
  trying to retake loopholes,
    73–74
  use of bayonet, 78
  vendetta against one
    commander, 64
  wounded, 65, 104
Lindhorst (Rifleman), 59, 74
  covering retreat, 80
Living Daylights The (Film), 125
Loading process for muskets/
  rifles, 40–41
Longford, Lady, 124

Lüneburg Light Battalion, 23, 33, 45, 47, 48, 49, 105, 106

Macintyre, Ben, xvi
*Marins (commander Second Battalion of 28th Ligne), 37
*Marrens (commander Second Battalion of 28th Ligne), 53, 102
Marriages, 14, 117
Martin, Lieutenant-Colonel David, 19
Mastnak, Jens, 131
Mauduit, Hippolyte, 56
Medics, 27, 53, 82. *See also* Gerson, Georg Hartog
Mevius (Sergeant-Major), 80
Meyer (Corporal), 6
Meyer, Lieutenant Christian, 96
Meyer, Lieutenant Georg, 26, 27, 36, 44, 80
    death of, 116
Meyer, Sergeant Diedrich, 50
Milius, Johan, 70
Mittelacher, Martin, 130–131
Mont-Saint Jean, 3, 11, 30
Morale
    Allied, 34, 105
    French, 29
    and troop cohesion, 105
Moreau (Ensign), 47
Müller, Corporal Henry, 45, 66, 80
Music, 14
Muskets
    loading process for muskets/ rifles, 40–41

musket vs. rifle firing rate/ accuracy, 40
problems with, 41–42

Nassauers, 22, 33, 72–73, 81, 95, 104, 106, 126
    and defence of Hougoumont, 130
NATO, 126, 128
Ney (Marshal), 30, 38, 58, 60, 83, 91, 121, 160(n2)
95th Rifles Regiment (British), 2, 5, 25, 28, 35, 52

Old Hubart, 17
Orange, Prince of, 23, 44, 87, 88, 127
    Butte de Lion mound in honour of, 122
Osborne, George, xvi

Pape, Fr., 48
Papelotte village, 22
Patriotism, xvii, 16, 108, 113
Pegot's brigade (French), 68–69, 77, 93
Pernet (French commander), 102
Physical exercise, 12
Picton, Lieutenant-General Thomas, 28, 44
    death of, 87, 124
Plancenoit village, 55, 69
Pontéecourlant (Lieutenant), 164(n21)
Poppe (Rifleman), 73
Prisoners, 64, 81, 91
Prussia, 10, 18, 119

Prussian forces, 1, 21, 30, 55, 57, 68, 69, 77, 92, 95, 123, 125

Pumphrey, Mary-Ann, 14, 34

Quatre Bras, battle of, 1, 3, 7, 22

Reese (Sergeant), 73, 74
Reille's 2nd Corps (French), 31, 33, 57, 104
Reinecke, Friedrich, 66
Religion, 108
Rhineland, 15
Richmond, Duchess of, 2
Riefkugel (Lieutenant), 96, 117
Riemstedt (Corporal), 59, 74
Riese, J., 48
Rifles, 118. *See also* Baker rifles
Rignon (French brigade commander), 53
Riotte, Torsten, 130
Robertson (Ensign), 27, 43, 96, 112
Roosevelt, Franklin Delano, xvii
Rossomme, 21
Rudersdorf, Jochem, 130–131
Russia, 10, 121

Sander (Rifleman), 45–46
Sandvoss, Philip, 74
Sappers, 32, 38, 58, 77
Sasse (Rifleman), 45
Schaumann (Captain), 26, 40, 42, 54
Scheldt, 11
Schläger, Lieutenant Charles, 118
Schlemm, Corporal Diedrich, 66

Schmidt, Sergeant-Major Ludwig, 47, 49
Schmitz's brigade, 37, 57
Schuck (Lieutenant), 85
Schüler, H., 48
Schwertfeger, Bernhard, 119, 164(n21)
2nd Battalion 28th/51st/105th Ligne (French), 102
2nd Light Battalion King's German Legion, 23, 91, 98, 113
and battle at Quatre Bras, 1
as bilingual, 13
casualties, 104 (*see also* Casualties: Allied)
on day after battle, 99
flag of, 47
forebears of Hanoverians in, 13
and German military tradition, 126
motivation of, xvii
patriotism of, xvii, 16, 108, 113
during period beginning12 years before battle, 9–10, 10–11
proportion of Hanoverians in, 10
as rearguard for entire allied army, 2
replacements for, 150(n5)
See also King's German Legion
Seven Years War, 13, 123
'Sharpe's Waterloo" (TV show), 124

Shaw (Corporal), 51
Shaw (Major), 98
Shaw-Kennedy (Captain), 84
Siborne, Captain William, 60–61,
    102, 120, 121, 129, 133
Simmons, Lieutenant George, 35
Skirmishers working in pairs, 66
Smith (Ensign), 96
Société belge d'études
    napoléoniennes, 122
Somerset (Lord), 51, 88
Southey, Robert, 102, 104
Spain, 20, 36, 108
Spörcken (Major), 27
Sports, 12
Square formations, 3, 46, 47, 48,
    49, 51, 54, 61, 62, 64, 69,
    71, 93, 107, 124–125
Stegen, Sergeant Wilhelm, 80
Stöckmann, Sergeant Georg, 47,
    64
Suicides, 116
Swedish Pomerania, 9

Tänzer, Michael-Andreas, 131
Taylor, John, 111
3rd British Infantry Division, 22
13th Light Infantry Regiment
    (French), 77
Thompson, Christopher, 130
Times, The, xvi
Timmann (Lieutenant), 96, 116
Tobin (Lieutenant), 26, 27, 36
    death of, 116
Trefcon, Colonel, 57
27th Infantry Regiment (Allied), 87
28th Line Regiment (French), 7,
    29

Ulstermen of the 27th
    Inniskillings, 84
Union Brigade, 130
'United nations', xvi–xvii

Vieux (Lieutenant), 43
von Alten, Charles (General), 12,
    13, 19, 20, 22, 23, 44, 46,
    87, 88, 118, 127
    account of battle by, 114
    as 'European soldier', 126
    honoured with statue of, 115
    injured, 93
von Brandis (Captain), 23, 46
von Dachsenhausen (ensign), 20
von dem Busche, Lieutenant-
    Colonel Louis, 22, 23, 27,
    42, 43, 48, 82, 155(n14)
von Einem (Major), 23, 93
von Gilsa (Captain), 45, 54, 85
von Hartmann, Sir Julius, 13,
    15–16
von Klenke (Lieutenant-General),
    47, 48, 49
von Linsingen (Lieutenant-
    Colonel), 71, 85–86, 89–90
von Marentholtz (Lieutenant),
    46–47
von Marschalck, Heinrich, 54, 85
von Ompteda, Oberstleutnant
    C. F., 115
von Ompteda, Christian, 17–19,
    22, 23, 24, 45, 61, 62, 70,
    71–72, 84, 85, 167(n5)
    and ammunition shortage,
    114
    command of 1st Light
    Battalion, 17

death of, 90–91, 98
horse felled by cannonball, 86
nephews of, 89–90, 118
and order to retake farmhouse, 88–89, 112, 126–127
von Ompteda, Christian Ludwig, 89–90, 118
von Ompteda, Captain August, 18
von Ompteda, Captain Ferdinand, 18
von Ompteda, Ludwig Albrecht, 89–90, 118
von Ompteda, Ludwig Karl Georg, 18
von Petersdorff (Major), 47
von Pflugk-Harttung, Julius, 119–120, 125, 133
von Schnehen, Major Wilhelm, 132
von Schröder, Lieutenant-Colonel, 22–23, 46
von Thurn und Taxis, Count August, 57–58
von Voigt (Captain), 46–47
von Weitershausen, (Captain), 72
von Westernhagen (Captain), 46–47
von Witte, Lieutenant Charles, 117–118
von Wurmb (Captain), 72

Walther (Ensign), 72
War of Spanish Succession, 123
Waterloo (film), 131
Waterloo, Battle of
British/Prussian controversy about, 114
centenary of, 120
as change in direction of the world, xv
climax of, 77
deployment of Allied forces, 22
French interest in, 121
as German victory, 125
'meeting one's Waterloo' concept, xv
panorama model of 1838, 102, 122–123
Waterloo Campaign, The. The German Victory (Hofschröer), 130
Waterloo Companion (Adkin), 130
Waterloo Dispatch (painting), 123
Waymouth (Lieutenant), 51
Weller, Jac, 129
Wellington, Duke of, xvi, 3, 21–22, 26, 44–45, 54, 57, 58, 69
and ammunition shortage, 77–78
'leave the Battle of Waterloo as it is', 129
mistakes made by, 102–103
number of men at disposal of, 30
as playing down Prussian contribution, 123
relations with troops, 108–109
Wellington's army as 'European', 125–126

Wheatley, Lieutenant Edmund,
16, 26, 62, 69, 77, 89,
90–91, 95, 97–98
marriage and death of, 117
taken prisoner, 91
Wiese, Corporal Wilhelm, 43,
68
Wilhelm II (Emperor), 119

Wilkie, Sir David, 123
Wishon, Mark, 130
Wittop, Sergeant Friedrich, 74
Witz, Wilhelm, 13
Women camp-followers, 26
World War I, 120, 125

Young Guard (French), 69